Corporate Governance in Banking

Nuggets from Canada, Georgia, Germany, U.K., and Zimbabwe

Justine Chinoperekweyi, Ph.D.

Foreword by: Dr. Abel C. Shimba

INDIA · SINGAPORE · MALAYSIA

Notion Press

Old No. 38, New No. 6
McNichols Road, Chetpet
Chennai - 600 031

First Published by Notion Press 2018
Copyright © Justine Chinoperekweyi 2018
All Rights Reserved.

ISBN 978-1-64429-146-7

To those who believe in the capacity of the modern corporation in transforming lives.

To those who believe in the power of sound corporate governance in economic transformation.

CONTENTS

ENDORSEMENTS

"My congratulations to Justine for addressing an important issue impacting many countries world-wide. Not only did he address the issues financial institutions are now facing but also offered a detailed plan of action on how to change. Thank you for your thoughtfully written chapter on Organization Development and providing such a clear description of what OD is, the importance of OD, and the requirements for effective organization development. I recommend this book to my colleagues and participants of our OD Certification Programs."

- **Dr. Nancy Zentis**

(Chief Strategist and CEO, Institute of Organization Development (IOD), Florida-USA)

"In my experience with Georgian banking sector, corporate governance is the key for the success of banks. I am honored to endorse Justine for writing about this vital pillar of banking sector - one of the biggest and most successful sectors in Georgia."

- **Ms. Tamara Bezhanishvili**

(Head of Internal Audit Department at JSC "ProCredit Bank" Georgia)

"This book written by Justine Chinoperekweyi is great, full of academic rigor and thorough in its coverage on corporate governance theories and best practices. It is well exemplified with case studies and guide readers prudently through different aspects of current corporate governance debates, not only for a specific region in Africa, but universally. This book is an essential (and much needed) addition to the body of knowledge of governance practitioners, academics, students and other related professionals. This multidisciplinary

book has taken an innovative approach as it is linking corporate governance with complexity theories as well as provides substantial new insights into why governance systems are failing and what may be done to improve this situation. Well done Justine for this great work. I endorse and recommend this book to all my colleagues and friends."

- **Mr. Kwanele Ngwenya**

(CEO, NBS Bank, Malawi)

"I am confident to endorse this book to young professionals in banking and in other fields of endeavor because I believe that the proposed measures for effective corporate governance are valuable to any organization in various settings. 'Moreso', I appreciate the inclusion of Chapter 9 on Organization Development (OD). Banks are organizations and they are governed and operated by people. The discussion of OD emphasizes the value of people even in financial institutions which highly deals with figures. OD is the bond that unifies human resource with the systems and structures and integrates an organization to becoming a relevant institution that will have a greater positive impact in society. I congratulate Dr. Justine for this book. I also pray that this book will empower many readers from around the world."

- **Roni Pedralvez**

(OD Specialist – Philippines)

"Justine addresses one of the most important issues of our times, the need for transformation of corporate governance in the financial industry worldwide. Justine masterfully connects the dots between a variety of theories, well-known real-case examples, the unpredictable factor of human nature, the importance of leadership, and how organization development can strengthen the whole organization. The many dimensions and the complexity of the whole subject are presented in a clear, structured and easy to follow style."

- **Nicole Heimann**

(CEO & Leadership Alliance Coach of Nicole Heimann & Partners AG, Switzerland)

"My congratulations to Justine for unpacking the importance of the global topical issue of corporate governance and its link to organizational performance. The chapter on Spirituality and Business Ethics in Corporate Governance brings in a new perspective in understanding organizational corporate governance. I recommend this book to my fellow academics, senior management and Board Members who are seized with articulating and upholding good corporate governance."

- **Dr. Takaruza Munyanyiwa**

(Adjunct Professor Apollos University (USA), Lecturer MSU (Zimbabwe), Organizational Leadership and Business Development Expert).

"Justine has unpacked important information for those of us who are passionate about Corporate Governance not only in banking industry but in all business institutions. Not only does the tone of this book cover banking in the countries that Justine writes about, but is relevant in the world over. Read this book - and learn from one of the best, if you still have conscience and believe in ethical leadership where you focus on "moral excellence, goodness, chastity and good character". Congratulations Justine."

- **Mrs. Avilla Dororosa Goba**

(Director Corporate Services; POTRAZ, Zimbabwe)

FOREWORD

I am pleased and privileged to endorse, "Corporate Governance in Banking: Nuggets from Canada, Georgia, Germany, U.K., and Zimbabwe." This book is a culmination of the author's years of research on the subject matter which he first presented as a doctoral thesis.

The importance of Corporate Governance in any organisation can never be over emphasized. Through this book Justine Chinoperekweyi approaches this subject squarely. He portrays that Corporate Governance is a necessary nutrient required for the success of any business that is exposed to today's dynamic and vibrant business environment. This is more so for the Banking Sector whose scope of operation has evolved over the years from the traditional deposit taking and cheque issuance to more complicated financial services. The convenience, efficiency and effectiveness in banking services brought about by innovations in the Banking sector has also brought about management challenges, some of which have resulted into Bank failures. Bank failures exert severe impact on the economy of a country and may result into the failure of more other banks. Between 1995 and 1997, Zambia my home country, experience the closure of about eight (8) Commercial Banks. The absence of sound Corporate Governance could be attributed to these closures. Thus, Justine Chinoperekweyi addresses a very important matter in this book.

Justine Chinoperekweyi has through this book demonstrated his passion and understanding of the principles of Corporate Governance as they relate to Banking. His intention is clear; that of educating, informing, inspiring and challenging leaders, managers, law makers, students, proprietors, e.t.c, to embrace sound management practices for the success their organizations. Reference made to real life examples of Bank failures in selected countries proves that these principles apply to the every organization and qualifies the book as a practical and sure guide to any goal driven manager or leader of any organisation.

Where there is no goal, people score anywhere (or people cannot score).

I hereby urge the reader to study this book and apply these principles in the operations of their organisation. The performance of your organisation will certainly change for the better. I therefore endorse this book.

Dr. Abel Chola Shimba, (Economist – Bank of Zambia).

ACKNOWLEDGMENTS

It takes the generosity of many people to write and publish any book. Many people contributed immensely to making this book a reality.

This book follows the completion of my doctoral thesis titled: *'Bank Failures: Examining corporate governance principles and practices of indigenous banks in Zimbabwe and their impact on organizational effectiveness'*. I therefore express my appreciation for the enormous intellectual support and guidance I received from The University of Lusaka (UNILUS) in Zambia and my two supervisors Dr. Emmanuel P. Mulenga and Dr. Abel C. Shimba.

Many thanks to my family and Wife (Grace) for being my hero, for inspiring and supporting always.

ABOUT THE AUTHOR

Justine Chinoperekweyi, Ph.D., is the author of the transformative books *Exceptionality Without Relapse: pathways and principles to creating an exceptional life*; and *Decision Making for Transformational Presence: Guide to making decisions that work.* Justine has a passion for teaching and championing true education and advancing the OD practice. He is involved in higher education and professional training and development as Director, Academic Director, Independent Speaker and Visiting Assistant Professor of Leadership & Finance in Zimbabwe and UAE. Justine is the Director & Academic Dean of Centre for Organization Leadership & Development (COLD) a competency-based vocational education & training institution.

Justine was born and brought up in Makoni District of Rusape in Zimbabwe. He can be contacted by email: justinechinz@yahoo.com.

INTRODUCTION

Times are changing for banking institutions and so is their governance. The changing times in the financial services space and the resultant complexity of corporate governance has brought about increased bank failures which to a greater extent informed the writing of this book. It is alleged that most of the bank failures that occurred since the beginning of the century has been a result of corporate governance deficiencies in these failed institutions. The need to determine the nature of corporate governance models in different jurisdictions and the determination of methods for optimal solutions cannot be overemphasized given the role of banks in economic transformation. This book reviews empirical and theoretical literature on banking sector corporate governance in order to determine methods of addressing corporate governance shortcomings in the financial sector.

Corporate governance is a key pillar in sustainability and it is imperative for every organization and economy to invest in strong corporate governance frameworks and practices in order to protect and grow wealth. Sound corporate governance frameworks help to identify gaps, outline areas of organizational reform, providing advice and assistance in corporate matters. Corporate governance can be defined from diverse dimensions, that is, as a philosophy of doing business; a set of mechanisms, procedures, and approaches for organizational effectiveness and methods to be sure that shareholder interests are correlated to the interests of managers. Literature indicates that there is a broad and narrow approach to defining corporate governance. The broad approach defines corporate governance with respect to all stakeholders whilst the narrow approach focuses on the maximization of shareholder wealth. The broad view incorporates institutional, legal, capacity building and rule of law whilst the narrow view focuses on internal processes, structure and rule of management within an institution.

Corporate governance is one of the crucial factors that support financial system stability in any country (Morck, Shleifer and Vishny, 1989). The roles of corporations vary depending on regional viewpoints (Rossouw, 2009). The variations have given rise to different corporate governance approaches in different countries. Corporate governance defined broadly refers to the relationship of the corporation to its society as a whole. Corporate governance is "the sum of the processes, structures and information used to direct and manage an organization" (Mayer, 1999). The essence of corporate governance is to create sustainable value or shared value which translates to profitability and embedded sustainability.

Knell (2006) suggests that governance involves controlling and regulating, that is, the exercise of authority to maintain order and adhere to predetermined standards of behavior. It is about developing and implementing processes and structures to ensure the organization is managed and directed in a manner that guarantees sustainable value to all shareholders, which will then enhance firm performance (Strine, 2010). During the past three decades, corporate governance has "evolved from the traditional 'profit centered model' (1900-1950) to the 'social responsibility model' (1950-1980)" (Halal, 2000). However, these two models are mutually exclusive since profit is fundamental to the survival of the firm. The firm's capacity to generate profit drives social impact investments in organizations (Shahin and Zairi, 2007). Currently corporate governance seems to be changing from the corporate social responsibility model towards collaborative working relations to be referred to as the "corporate community model" (Halal, 2000); and the incorporation of Artificial Intelligence (AI), particularly computational ethics in corporate governance mechanisms.

The adoption of the corporate community model is essential in creating shared value which takes into consideration all the stakeholders of the company thereby ensuring inclusive effectiveness. This model is also founded on complexity science. Complexity science offers that all organizations are relatively complex, and the complexity that arises is not necessarily the result of various agents interacting in a complex way; rather, complex behavior of the whole can be the result of both the number of coupled agents and the diversity of interaction of these interconnections. Business organizations have been greatly criticized as the major cause of environmental, social, and economic challenges. As complex adaptive systems, it is therefore imperative for organizations to redefine their purpose as "creating shared value". Shared value involves the firm's attempts to create economic value in a way that optimizes value for all stakeholders (Porter and Kramer, 2011). The widespread reliance on machine intelligence is also reshaping the approaches to corporate governance.

The governance of banking institutions is increasingly becoming complex due to the increasing pace of globalization in financial markets, the emergence of conglomerate corporate structures, offshore accounts, technology and innovations in financial products and services. In view of the emergence of financial technology companies (FinTech), a wave of convergence in the banking market has altered the manner in which banks should be governed. The banking sector of today is extremely segmented as compared to banking in the previous centuries. The changing times has given contemporary banking institutions significant economies of scale and scope. Banking institutions are becoming progressively more diversified, offering an expanding variety of services and financial products. The banking operating environment is also influenced by the increasing number of market infrastructure providers and global technology companies which are defining, redefining and disrupting the nature of banking.

Despite the developments in the banking and financial services space, the sector is drawn at the centre of the causes of the 2008/09 global financial crisis and other crises. The corporate governance deficiencies in banks led to these crises. The enormous impact of the global financial crisis has raised regulatory alarms globally. This rise has necessitated the increased focus on corporate governance. The stability and solvency of the banking sector depends on the quality of corporate governance in an economy. The banking sector is considered the engine of economic transformation as providers of credit and facilitators of the payment system. The banking industry in most economies suffers from the problem of distress and bankruptcy, which ultimately affects all other sectors due to the important financial intermediation role of banks. Good corporate governance has become quintessential for enhancing organizational effectiveness, inspiring investors, strengthening investor rights, and encouraging economic transformation. It is worrisome to note that despite increased attention to corporate governance in almost all economies, most countries still exhibit poor corporate governance credentials as shown by the relative poor performance of most organizations in these economies. Various scholars and corporate governance practitioners alleged that the poor corporate governance credential in most countries are a result of corruption, weak regulatory frameworks, lack of shareholder sophistication, and other macro-environmental influences.

In view of the multi-dimensional effect of bank failures, specifically on the various sectors of the economy; the ramifications of failure are unacceptably costly to any economy. It is against this background that this book tackles banking sector corporate governance issues from a complexity science perspective and using case study approach of different countries. In simple terms, bank failure refers to a situation when a bank cannot effectively perform its core activities. The banking sector is highly susceptible to the epidemic of inadequate corporate governance and this negatively affects organizational effectiveness as measured through profitability, growth and sustainability in order to build resilient economies. The negative effects of one institution affect system stability and solvency and eventually the whole economy. The quality of corporate governance expected of banking institutions in the current business environment is high.

It is essential to recognize that corporations, particularly banks, have become stronger entities in modern economies due to the surge of capitalism, and most governments had to succumb to the corporate sector's manipulation and dominance. The number of banking institutions in many economies has increased greatly since the beginning of the 21st century, and people have grown so accustomed to them such that their existence, functions, and continued operations are often taken for granted. "Banks are strange beasts." It is extremely crucial for people at all levels to understand how banks are governed and the difference between their governance and that of other firms. An understanding of the effects of the bank's corporate structures on organizational effectiveness is equally important across all stakeholders.

The gist of this book is to help readers enhance their understanding of corporate governance in banking institutions; in view of the complex, disruptive and wrenching macro and micro environmental changes. Governance of companies in the era of knowledge society and disruptive technological change has become as important for the global economy as the governance of countries. Promoting sound corporate governance practices help in developing the pillars of an effective business environment that is conducive for innovation and growth. Transformation of the modern society and the countless productive enterprises is central to a sustainable economy. This is where governance translates to organizational longevity which in turn allows enterprises to evolve and grow. Banks play an important role in the evolution and growth of all other enterprises.

In view of systems thinking, the term institution is purposely used in this book as it denotes special sound corporate governance characteristics: prescription of norms of behavior, their relevant permanence independent of individuals, and their applicability in the entire society. An institution is defined as an organization imbued with a mission to make an impact on the society. Banks should be model institutions, hence the increased attention given to their governance. This book reviews certain corporate governance nuggets from different countries in order to devise corporate governance informed methods of optimal solutions for banks and the corporate sector at large. Based on the view of banks as complex adaptive systems, the review therefore helps to crystallize the essential methods of optimal solutions in the governance of banks going into the future.

In order to accommodate all the banking sector stakeholders, this book takes an enterprise governance approach; which emphasizes corporate governance conformance and performance in an organization's life. The adoption of the enterprise governance approach is in response to the devastating effects of the Global Financial Crisis 2008/09 that resulted from the seemingly exclusive focus on the conformance dimension. The exclusive focus on the conformance dimension has led to an exponential increase in the number of laws, regulations and guidelines directed at organizations (McConvill, 2005). The integration of corporate governance conformance and performance is considered essential in determining strategic complexity and the solvency and stability of banks in different countries and also to crystallize the elements that the future governance model need to incorporate. The conformance dimension is addressed through codes and standards, with compliance being subject to assurance and audit. Conformance takes a historic view to governance and covers corporate governance issues such as chairman and CEO roles, role and composition of the board, board committees, controls assurance, regulatory authorities, and risk management for compliance. The performance dimension takes a forward-looking perspective and is focused on strategy and value creation. The primary focus of the performance dimension of corporate governance is on helping organizations make strategic decisions, understand risk appetite and key performance drivers. The enterprise governance approach therefore favors the corporate community model of governance which covers all corporate governance actors in drawing out governance mechanisms.

WHAT IS BANKING?

To be able to understand the uniqueness of banking corporate governance it is important to grasp the meaning and importance of banks. *Why do banks exist? Can the modern economy function without banking institutions?* Banking has a long and honorable history. Scholarly articles indicate that the term bank is derived from the Greek word *trapeza* which designates the balance that early money changers used to weigh coins in order to determine the exact quantity of precious metals the coins contained. The Italian word for bank is derived from the Italian merchants' bench, or *banco*, on which money changed hands in the marketplaces of medieval Italy. Bankruptcy refers to the "breaking of the bench" that occurred when the Italian merchant banker over-extended, then experienced a run on his notes, and failed.

Traditionally, the three key features of banking business were: taking deposits from customers and maintaining accounts on their behalf; managing payments on behalf of customers through collecting and paying cheques, notes and other 'banking currency'; and advancing loans to customers. Sustainability in modern operating environment requires banks to be integrative and structured in performing banking functions. Contemporary banking theory classifies banking functions into four broad categories. First, banks offer liquidity and settlement services. These include exchange, deposit management, safekeeping and payment service. Second, banks are involved in transforming assets. Asset transformation includes the creation of mutual fund and insurance activities. Third, banks manage risks and allow investors to diversify their risk and hold portfolios of financial assets. Finally, banks are involved in processing information and monitoring borrowers. From the vantage point of Adam Smith, the existence of financial intermediaries is attributed to market imperfections. Banks therefore exist to reduce transactions, search, monitoring, and information costs because all financial transactions entail costs for all the participants in the market. Banks have also entered the new advisory roles, providing help and advice to other businesses for fee income.

Banking encompasses banks and other financial intermediaries. These are institutions that accept deposits and redeploy those funds by investing in financial assets. Banks are the principal caretakers of the economy's money supply and provide important source of funds for consumers and businesses. An appropriate banking environment is a key pillar as well as an enabler of economic transformation (Koivu, 2000). The critical financial intermediary role that banks plays in economic transformation necessitates special corporate governance treatment. The corporate governance justification for banks is also founded on the fact that banks finance a significant fraction of their loans through the deposits of the public. Corporate governance therefore plays a role of safeguarding customer wealth. Banks are unique businesses, not only as guarantors of deposits, but also as suppliers of capital (Chagwiza, 2012). The governance of banking institutions is therefore a strategic imperative for economic transformation.

THE DISTINCTIVE CHARACTERISTICS OF BANKS: AN EMPIRICAL REVIEW

Real sector firms are mainly funded through owners' funds. Banks are however unique in that most of the bank's capital is raised through deposit accumulation hence the increased probability of excessive risk taking by banks. The intermediary's incentive for excessive risk taking is necessitated by the fact that high-risk investments most likely generate increased revenues, while if the investment fails most of the costs will be borne by the depositors. Bank shareholders, directors and bank managers therefore assume greater fiduciary responsibilities as a result of raising public deposits. This is because all depositors' funds need to be safeguarded in a special way in order to ensure financial sector stability and solvency. The capital structure of banks comprises more debt than equity, as a result of the reliance on deposit accumulation. The agency problem in banking is therefore more complicated as a result of the simultaneous divergence in interests and risk perception among several contracting parties. However, dispersed depositors have little incentive to monitor bank operations due to the free-riding problem.

In addition, increased information asymmetry and coordination costs discourage the monitoring of bank managers and equity owners by depositors (Demirguc-Kunt and Detragiache, 2002). The system of deposit insurance is therefore used to protect depositors. However, the deposit insurance provides intermediaries with stronger incentives for risky behavior (Merton, 1977). On the other hand, protected depositors are less-sensitive to bank risk as compared to institutional and other investors. As a result, depositors do not demand adequate compensation for bank risk taking which makes debt a cheap source of funds and biases banks toward it (Mehran *et al.*, 2011). Therefore, banks are much more leveraged than real sector firms (Acharya *et al.*, 2009). Depositors find it difficult to determine the true value of a bank's loan portfolio at any specific time. This is because such information is incommunicable and very costly to reveal (Bhattacharya *et al.*, 1998). The role of bank deposits has varied over time, yet they remain the optimal form of funding for banks across the globe (Diamond, 1984).

According to Mehran *et al.*, (2011), banks also have many stakeholders than non-financial firms. Bank stakeholders include debt holders, mainly depositors and the holders of subordinated debt. The deposit insurance authority is another key banking sector stakeholder because the insurance funds will be called upon in the case of insolvency. The board of directors, in spite of the multitude of stakeholders, solely represents the views of shareholders, in the context of regulatory constraints. Conflict of interests between shareholder and other stakeholders in banking is inevitable especially on risk, where shareholders prefer volatility and may have short-term perspectives. In most cases, debt holders and regulators prefer long-term perspectives and low volatility.

Banks are highly opaque and complex. The opaqueness of banks is explained by the degree of information asymmetry between inside and outside investors (Harris and Raviv, 1991). There has been an increasing theoretical literature justifying the conventional wisdom on the informationally opaqueness of banks (Diamond, 1991; Kwan and Carleton, 1998). As Levine (2004) notes, "banks can alter the risk composition of their assets more quickly than most non-financial industries, and banks can readily hide problems by extending loans to clients that cannot service previous debt obligations." In essence, the business of securitization plays two main roles:

- accelerating the lending process at the origination stage and in interbank markets, and
- increasing opacity by consolidating large amounts of information and relying on credit ratings. Bank opacity reduces market discipline and encourages banks to take too much risk. Bank opacity refers to the extent of uncertainty about banks' risk exposure (Mishkin, 2000).

Banking opacity and complexity is essential in the interaction between the board and management. It also plays a significant role in the relationship between the bank and regulators. The complexity of banking makes the challenges involved in their corporate governance highly specific. "The complexity of the banking business increases the asymmetry of information and diminishes stakeholders' capacity to monitor bank managers' decisions" (Andres and Vallelado, 2008).

Corporate governance of banking institutions is of greater importance given the crucial financial intermediation role of banks in economy and is essential to achieving and maintaining public trust and confidence in the banking system (The Basel Committee, 2008). As the main intermediaries in the financial system, banks are important engines of economic growth (King and Levine, 1993). Banks are active contributors to industrial expansion, the corporate governance of real firms, and the allocation of capital.

Banks play a critical role in describing and prescribing the corporate governance of other firms (Franks and Mayer, 2001); as creditors or equity holders (Santos and Rumble, 2006). The failure of banks may be highly costly and unacceptable due to their special financial intermediation role and management of the payment system (Haan and Vlahu, 2013). In this regard, excessive risk-taking by banks creates significant negative externalities and systemic risk hence the heavy regulation of the financial sector as compared to non-financial sectors (Flannery, 1998). The ability of banks to efficiently mobilize deposits and allocate funds is essential in lowering the cost of capital to firms, increasing capital formation, and stimulating productivity growth. Therefore, the stability of the banking sector through effective governance; sector regulation, and supervision becomes vital.

Banks play a decisive role in decreasing the informal economy and increasing the transparent operations of the companies through bank accounts. Banks are regarded as strange beasts. "Much like electrical utilities or railroads, they are private-sector firms whose healthy functioning is in the public interest" (McGlaughlin and Mehran, 1995). Banking, it would seem, is too important to leave entirely to bankers (Mehran and Mollineaux, 2012).

Historical examples of a frozen financial system and bank runs or silent runs depositors underscore the need for healthy financial markets. Deadweight losses to the economy can come from both idiosyncratic and systemic failures in the financial system. Numerous scholars have documented the links between finance and growth in all economies (King and Levine, 1993; Rajan and Zingales, 1998). According to Levine (1997), a strong financial system provides five main services:

- facilitating production and distribution of goods and services though managing the payments system,
- supervising and disciplining borrowers,
- investments appraisal and advisory,
- managing risk and uncertainty, and
- mobilizing savings for investment.

MEANING OF CORPORATE GOVERNANCE

Corporate governance is a uniquely complex and multifaceted subject which has assumed increased attention as a policy, academic and strategic issue. Literature and history points out that though the subject of corporate governance lacks a cohesive theory; its paradigm, diagnosis and solutions lie in various fields such as psychology, business, economics and law. Any analysis of corporate governance should be guided by contemporary business practices, psychology, economics and law in a range of national systems. Corporate governance is leadership for creating and sustaining institutions. It is the key factor that determines the health and ability of organizations to survive environmental shocks and win in the complex, disruptive and wrenching business environment.

Corporate governance determines the soundness and connectedness of the individual components of an organization and the elements of the external environment. It is a method of aligning the internal and external business environment in order to further the business goals. It refers to the extent to which the internal stakeholders of the firm adopt leadership in order to build an effective organization. Corporate governance incorporates reporting, compliance with legislation and statutory regulations, accountability, transparency and fairness. It also encompasses positioning companies to interactively make robust strategic decisions and manage risks. According to the OECD, the four pillars of corporate governance are: fairness, accountability, independence, and transparency. The OECD Principles of Corporate Governance are based on these four pillars of corporate governance.

Corporate governance is both the structure and relationships which determine corporate efficiency, direction and performance for the benefit of all stakeholders and the sustainability of the corporation. The board of directors is central to corporate governance due to its oversight role in strategic thinking and strategic leadership. However, the importance of management and employees in corporate sustainability cannot be overemphasized. In broad terms, literature has defined corporate governance as the way in which a corporation is directed, administered and controlled. It involves the process of decision making and the process by which corporate decisions may be implemented. These processes demand that an organization adopts methods of optimal solutions. The difference between corporate management and corporate governance indicate the shift to support the changing times and the need to be strategic when dealing with the complex corporate issues. Organizations cannot exclusively rely on scientific management, bureaucratic management and Hawthorne approaches in management. However, these two corporate functions are mutually exclusive and demands equal attention in organizational life.

From a banking sector perspective, corporate governance involves:

- Setting banking strategies and objectives. This focuses on the development of the overall strategic intent and service strategy of the bank. The setting of the bank's strategic intent determines corporate direction and should adopt a stakeholder perspective. The service strategy should be aligned to the overall strategic intent.
- Setting the bank's risk tolerance or appetite in the context of the volatile, uncertain, and ambiguous operating environment. This demands a strong, integrative, holistic and structured risk governance approach.
- Operate the bank's business on a day-to-day basis. This approach should be aligned with the overall corporate direction and strategy.

Good corporate governance considers the organization as a system or network, and as such is a necessary tool for creating and sustaining superior performance. From the vantage point of The McKinsey 7s framework, the internal environment comprises the 'hard' and the 'soft' 7s: strategy, structure, systems, staff, skills, style, and shared values. These internal environment elements should be aligned to the broader macro-environment in order to ensure the sustainability and profitability of the business. Corporate governance is about putting companies in a position to make robust strategic decisions and manage risks. In the absence of sound corporate governance, there is a scope of unethical practices which threaten the success of an organization due to the agency problem and the ensuing agency costs. Banking is highly susceptible to unethical practices, and as such upholding to the highest levels of ethical practices is a strategic priority. An organization should be governed in line with the going concern principle, hence the significance of corporate governance in enhancing the sustainability and profitability of bank operations.

There has been a number of bank failures in most economies despite sophisticated risk management methodologies, increased bank regulations, and the existence of seemingly competent boards, senior executives, and professional managers. Increasing globalization of financial markets, emergence of conglomerate structures, offshore accounts, input of new technological structures and disruptive financial products innovation have added to the complexity of corporate governance in banking and financial services sector. The emergence of globalization has led to greater deterritorialization and less governmental control, hence the need for greater accountability at organizational level (Crane and Matten, 2007). In view of the increased number of bank failures, there are two main questions that form the foundation of this book. *Why have such failures occurred? What might have been done differently to prevent such failures?* The answers to these questions are closely linked to corporate governance shortcomings, hence the need to determine methods of optimal bank corporate governance solutions premised on Organization Development (OD) theory and practice.

The bank failure case studies below illustrate that though corporate governance failings were not the only cause of bank failures, they were significant. These case studies aim to discover common ground across different episodes of bank failures in Canada, Germany, United States of America, United Kingdom, and Zimbabwe.

BANK FAILURE CASE STUDIES

Below is a review of the bank failure case studies in Canada, Germany, United States of America, United Kingdom, and Zimbabwe. These case studies form the foundation of all the succeeding chapters of this book.

INTEGRITY BANK – UNITED STATES OF AMERICA (2000-2008)

Integrity Bank of Alpharetta, Ga., was opened in November 2000 as a specialist real estate lending bank, and became the fastest growing bank in the country. The bank was based in Florida but had its fortunes tied in Alpharetta, Ga. The bank failed in August 2008 and the failure did cost the United States (US) deposit insurance fund over $295 million. The failure of Integrity Bank was primarily a result of the bank's concentration of real estate development loans to a single borrower. The bank was overexposed to Mr. Guy Mitchell the owner of Casa Madonna Hotel & Spa. This was in violation of the country's law which prohibited banks from lending more than 25% of their capital into a single borrower. Unacceptably costly deficiencies were recorded in the bank's credit division, as loan facilities were not properly approved and credit underwriting was lacking. Almost 50% of the bank's $668.4 million construction loans were non-performing at the end of Q2 (2008). The bank also made numerous loans for a total of $83 million to one borrower. Bank regulators indicated that Integrity Bank's compensation policy rewarded external competencies; hence executives took high risks because they earned commission based on loan volume, and not loan portfolio quality. The executives also received kickbacks from customers upon loan approval.

Besides the bad loan portfolio, falling real estate values and inadequate risk management; Integrity Bank's board was marked by infighting and high turnover among senior executives. According to the Herald-Tribune Investigation, "The bank had five presidents in its first four years. It also went for an entire year without a CEO and ultimately promoted its Chief Lending Officer, who had no experience managing a bank." Due to dissent among members of the board of directors, six out of ten members of the board resigned in December 2007.

Founded on Christian principles, Integrity Bank used the motto "*In God We Trust*". The bank gave customers free Bibles, and employees prayed together at meetings. The executives failed to live up to the bank's name or mission.

HOME BANK OF CANADA (HBC) (1903-1923)

A white cardboard placard scrawled with "*Bank closed. Payments suspended*" was nailed to the door of HBC head office on 17 August 1923. One of the bank's managers was quoted saying "on the way down (to an urgent management meeting) I heard rumors that the bank has failed. We have heard nothing of this in my branch. We have been doing a splendid business. I can't understand it." The failure of HBC impacted on over 60,000 depositors. HBC had over 70 branches and its board of directors included esteemed members of the business community. The bank reported 'profits' two months before its suspension.

James Mason was the president of HBC at the time of its collapse. It is alleged, Mason extended loans to entrepreneur and real estate speculator Sir Henry Pellatt who happened to be a close family friend. Loans were also extended to companies with which Mason and other directors were intimately involved. This led to an increase in non-performing loans, yet HBC officers kept approving additional loan facilities, and the accruing interest of the accounts was capitalized on the principal. This bit of creative or fraudulent accounting enabled the bank to paint the financial picture as much rosier than it was, and to issue shareholders dividends (at 7% per annum) on the basis of this 'profit'. In 1914 William Machaffie (HBC Branch Manager) got fired for alerting the directors of this creative accounting (cooking the books of accounts). The HBC board never cared to closely examine the books and trusted Mason's stewardship. HBC audits were performed by the firm's loyal and untrained auditors.

HERSTATT BANK - GERMANY (1956-1974)

Herstatt Bank (HB) was a small bank, and the 35th biggest bank in Germany. Its failure should have been a parochial affair yet the failure received much attention in international finance. The case of HB was the largest and most spectacular failure in Germany banking history. HB failure precipitated a chain reaction across financial centers because the bank had important international connections due to its foreign exchange trading. This made its failure the "worst bank collapse" since the crisis of 1931 in Germany. Herstatt Bank got into trouble because of its large and risky foreign exchange business. The bank had a high concentration of activities in the area of foreign trade payments. HB's failure was due to its speculation on the foreign exchange markets. The collapse of the Bretton Woods System in March 1973, the free floating of currencies provided HB with additional incentives for risky exchange bets.

Danny Patel was the head of the foreign exchange division and the department used to work to a larger extent without control and with little contact to other divisions. Iwan Herstatt, who was the bank's president clearly left a lot of freedom to the foreign currency division. This relaxed attitude by Iwan Herstatt posed problems for the German Banking Supervisor (BAKred), since BAKred *(Bundesaufsichtsamt fur das Kreditwesen)* was at regular intervals getting in touch with only one person in the bank. The failure of HB caused more bank failures, particularly on banks whom Herstatt owed delivery of foreign currencies. This brought about the Herstatt risk. The foreign exchange exposure of the bank was estimated to be 80 times more than its exposure limit. The foreign exchange risk was estimated to be three (3) times as large as the amount of the bank's capital. Faulty forecasting and lax internal regulation resulted in extremely high exposure levels. The New York interbank market came to a standstill almost leading to the collapse of other institutions. Shortly after the event, Peter Cooke from Bank of England (BoE) proposed setting up a committee of central banks and supervisory authorities, which became known as the Basel Committee. HB's failure made it an eponymous bank failure.

FRANKLIN NATIONAL BANK – LONG ISLANDS (1926-1974)

Franklin National Bank (FNB) had been one of the most profitable banks in Long Island. FNB was a powerful stimulus to the region's sub-urban growth and commercial development. The founder, Arthur T. Roth was one of the Long Island's most revered business and civic leaders. The FNB failure altered US banking regulations and global financial practices. The key question is: *What brought Franklin down?* "Explanations range from dry statistical analyses of the economy and Franklin's own books to charges of autocracy, over-ambition, personal betrayal and international skullduggery." Tom Murphy, FNB Supervisor, was quoted saying; "The bank was in good shape in 1968 – 110%." Arthur T. Roth wrote that "Franklin's operations were "unsatisfactorily minus", cause: incompetence stemming from the top, negligence of directors to take full remedial action, lack of full disciplinary action of supervisory authorities."

The FNB demise was unique because federal regulators orchestrated the bank's winding down its operations in order to prevent global economic damage (an economic hit). FNB's 1974 hemorrhage cash situation arose because of high risk loans, ill-advised foreign currency transactions and swings in foreign exchange rates. Joan Spero probed in *The Failure of FNB*, the entangled mess of greed, deception, and mismanagement that brought about the downfall of FNB.

BARINGS BANK – UNITED KINGDOM (1762-1995)

Age is just a number in corporate life. Even the giants, like the biblical Goliath, can collapse from the sling shot of one man. *'Barings Bank goes bust.'* Barings Bank was the oldest merchant bank in the UK before its spectacular collapse in 1995. The collapse of the 233 years old Barings was caused by one man. The key question is: *How can one man single-handedly bankrupt a 233 years old bank?* Barings was so distinguished that it did not have any logo, it had a crest. The Barings demise was caused by the rogue, brilliant and most confident trader Nicholas William Leeson. Leeson stated that "the ethos at Barings were simple, we were all driven to make profits, profits and more profits...it was the rising star." Leeson helped Barings make vast sums of money, for example in 1993, he made £10 million – 10% of the bank's profits for the year. However, the executionary approach to management exposed Barings, leading to the bank's collapse.

In 1995, Barings discovered the secret file – Error Account 88888 which was used to facilitate Leeson's surreptitious trading. The account showed Leeson had gambled away £827 million in Barings name. The fall of Barings was attributed to 'unauthorized and concealed trading positions', and serious problems of controls and management failings within the Barings Group. *Who was Nicholas William Leeson in Barings Bank?* Leeson doubled as Assistant Director and General Manager of Barings Futures Singapore (BFS) and took charge of both the trading floor *(front office)* and transactions settlement operations *(back office)*. This enabled him to make seismic bets on the Japanese markets and hide his losses and unauthorized trading using the 88888 Account. The audit function was weak as it failed to ask critical questions after the 19 July 1994 – August 1994 internal audit, and the January 1995 discovery of discrepancies in the BFS accounts by the senior auditors. The Barings failure shows how hubris, weak oversight, and lack of internal controls can bring an organization down. The devastating Kobe earthquake of 17 January 1995 caused $100 billion in damage or 2.5% of Japan's Gross Domestic Product (GDP). This eventually shook the bond and stock markets and Leeson's losses ballooned to £827 million and he was no longer able to disguise them from Barings management.

RENAISSANCE MERCHANT BANK LIMITED – ZIMBABWE (2006-2011)

The financially-beleaguered ReNaissance Merchant Bank (RMB) was placed under curatorship for six months on the 2nd of June 2011. The Reserve Bank of Zimbabwe had established systematic abuse of depositors' funds, a high level of non-performing insider loans and related party exposures including a $9.8 million loan to the former CEO Paterson Timba. Gross violations of banking laws and regulations were recorded. RMB was technically insolvent with a negative capital of $16.7 million against the prescribed minimum capital requirement of $10 million for merchant banks as at April 30, 2011. Non-performing loans constituted 38% of the total loan book of which the bulk were loans to insiders. The three founding directors of RMB had a total interest of 78.03% in the bank. Collectively executive management owned about 89.17% of the Group's shareholding. Patterson Timba irregularly 'borrowed' depositors' funds to finance personal business interests and acquisitions. There was no separation between shareholders, board and management. The bank also suffered from liquidity problems due to speculation and engaging in non-core activities. The failure of RMB can be summed up as due to ill-planned expansion drives not synchronized with the overall strategic initiatives, 'corporate incest', ill-equipped management, inadequate risk management systems, undue influence or dominance by a few shareholders, poor corporate governance structures, and improperly constituted board structures.

The examples of bank failures profiled above illustrate a number of corporate governance deficiencies in the way banks were or are being directed and managed. These failures advertise the lack of effective internal controls, the folly of trusting one employee, lack of board oversight, shareholder domination, poor risk management, compensation systems that exclusively focus on rewarding external competencies and lack of employee engagement and corporate reporting deficiencies. There is therefore a need to inquire and implement methods of optimal solutions. The profiled case studies do cast a dark shadow on the reliance on a rules-based approach to corporate governance. The issues explicitly and implicitly stated in the case studies seem to be prevalent in the present banking business.

CORPORATE GOVERNANCE AND BANK FAILURES

The devastating effects of the East Asian crisis and other crises led to the heightened interest about the role of bank weaknesses in contributing to systemic banking crises. The role of corporate governance in the stability of banking institutions and subsequently the overall economy cannot be overemphasized. The widespread financial distress in almost all economies during the last three decades has raised concerns on the way banks are being managed and directed. The prevalence of banking crises advertises the enormous consequences of poor corporate governance. Banking crises have the enormous effects of crippling economies, destabilizing governments and intensifying poverty (Levine, 1999). Banks are fragile and highly susceptible to panic.

Banking system fragility emanates from sector-specific uncertainty factor and uneven competitive structure (Basu, 2003). The main source of banking sector panics are speculative attacks on the *numeraire*, information asymmetry between banks, depositors and other stakeholders. Information asymmetry is a situation in which one part to a contract or agreement has more information as compared to another. Banks are highly susceptible to unwarranted withdrawals of deposits during banking panic episodes. A lack of depositor confidence leads to unwarranted withdrawals. Depositor confidence is a measure of trust that the bank customers have over the banking system of an economy. Systemic bank runs occur because depositors believe that others depositors will run, hence depositors imitate each other's withdrawal behavior. This can lead to a bank failure, that is, a bankrupt or busted bank. Examples include Pre-World War 1 banking panics in US (1857-1907) and events during the Great Depression, including the Chicago banking panic of June 1932.

The bank failures of 1875-1913 were a result of an increase in the liabilities of failed banks by more than 50% and a decline by more than 8% on the stock market. Bank failures in the 1830s, 1850s, and 1920s were a result of significant macroeconomic contraction. Large fundamental problems that had their sources in government-induced shocks to the money supply led to the 1830s bank failures (Rousseau, 2002). Other causes of these banking panic episodes included unprofitable bank financed infrastructure investments (Schweikart, 1987), and international balance of payments shocks (Temin, 1969). Fundamental problems, such as collapses of agricultural prices led to the 1920s agricultural bank failures (Calomiris, 1992).

Silent runs and bank walks are more common modes of bank failures in contemporary banking. Due to the complexity of the banking environment, silent runs are more prevalent. A silent run is a slow-motion bank run, in which bank customers do not demand all their money immediately, but curtail making fresh deposits to replenish their withdrawals. This gradually pushes the bank beyond its capitalization breaking point. This is especially gravitating to banks as the hassle and cost of serving customers remains, but the vast bulk of the deposits are gone. Bank walks happens when large depositors feel a rush of bank runs is imminent, hence depositors will distribute deposits in separate bank accounts.

In view of the enterprise governance model and systems thinking, this book therefore targets all banking sector stakeholders in order to enhance understanding of the fundamental corporate governance concepts and elements that should be incorporated in the future governance model of banks. The book provides constructive insights for those in the academia, organization development practitioners, and corporate governance practitioners. The book is also a useful guide to the next generation leaders and mission-critical managers in not only banking but across sectors. Though the book might not be exhaustive, it represents an attempt to reveal corporate governance deficiencies in the banking sector.

CHAPTER 1

THEORIES OF CORPORATE GOVERNANCE &

CORPORATE GOVERNANCE CODES

To assess the corporate governance of banks, one needs a thorough understanding of relevant concepts. There are diverging views on the concept and origins of corporate governance. The theories underlying the development of corporate governance and the areas it encompasses date from much earlier and is drawn from a number of disciplines.

Berle and Means (1932) introduced the modern theory of corporate governance. Some scholars are of the view that the roots of corporate governance ideas stretch back to the 1890s (Wells, 2010). Corporate governance development is a global occurrence and as such, is a complex area including legal, cultural, ownership and other structural differences. The development of an effective corporate governance framework requires an understanding of the existing differences and facts attached to it. The evolution of corporate governance has had trends, themes and models. Corporate direction and corporate control are the two cornerstones of the corporate governance system. History reveals the never-ending evolution of corporate governance models as necessitated by the minimal essence of social consciences and the rise in the profit-making narrative. Companies across the globe are trying to instill the sense of sound corporate governance into their corporate structures (Abdullah and Valentine, 2009). The modern corporation has become a powerful and dominant institution hence the heightened importance of corporate governance.

The modern corporation is a powerful and dominant institution due to its capabilities and influences; for example, the role of banks in transforming assets, information, and people. The corporate governance of the modern corporation significantly influences economies and various aspects of social landscape. The shareholder primacy model and the stakeholder primacy model are the predominant corporate governance models. Stephen Bainbridge (2008) developed the director primacy model which views directors as having control of the firm and the "ultimate right to fiat". The main theories that have affected the development of corporate governance in banking and probably all other sectors are agency theory, stakeholder theory, transaction cost theory, managerial-hegemony theory and stewardship theory.

AGENCY THEORY

This theory has its roots in economic theory as exposited by Alchian and Demsetz (1972) and Jensen and Meckling (1976). The agency theory is founded on the belief that the separation of ownership and control amplifies the opportunity for management to take action for their own benefit, and at the expense of shareholders and other stakeholders. This is referred to as the agency problem and the costs borne by the shareholders and other stakeholders are known as agency costs. Agents view all stakeholders as irrelevant-opportunists and their benefitting from the business is coincidental to the management's activities in running the business to serve the shareholders. The agent may succumb to self-dealing, opportunistic behaviour and falling short of congruence between the aspirations of the principal and the agent's pursuits. Managers are considered to be atomistic and self-serving agents.

Corporate governance is therefore a control and oversight system to lessen agency costs. It is a set of mechanisms, procedures and approaches to safeguard shareholder and stakeholders' interests. Agency problem emanates from the divergent goals of cooperating parties in an organization. Eisenhardt (1989) purports that the agency theory deals with the 'ubiquitous agency relationship' in which the principal delegates responsibilities to the agent, who will perform according to their capacity. The assumption is that because agents do not own firm's resources they might carry out moral hazards in order to enhance their wealth at the cost of principals. The two main sources of agency conflicts are:

- Imperfect information which arises when the agent has access to more and better information about the business and the respective interests between the parties are not perfectly symmetrical. The principal cannot supervise adequately the agent's actions.
- Misaligned incentives between the principal and agent due to the impossibility of having perfectly aligned interests between the principal and agent because 'random factors may influence the agent's output' (Alexander, 2006).

The conflict between principals (shareholders) and agents (managers) lead to adverse selection and moral hazard. The former is a situation where the agent exploits the information asymmetry that exists and 'determines the appropriateness of the agent's actions but which are imperfectly observable by others (Alexander, 2006). It occurs when there is lack of symmetric information to a deal. This represents a form of 'pre-contractual opportunism'. The agent's information dominance is created by the impossibility of full information disclosure between the agent and principal, and puts the principal in the situation of relying mostly on proxy information. The latter is a situation where the agent pursues his/her self-interest at the cost of the principal by following a different track that principal's preference. This is regarded as 'post-contractual opportunism', linked to hidden actions, which cannot be accurately followed, making impossible to condition contracts on these actions (Alexander, 2006).

3

The traditional view of the agency theory indicates that the corporate governance mechanisms have as a target the alignment of managers' interests with those of shareholders, in order to avoid high risk-taking incentives for managers. The main characteristic of the governance problem is the possibility of managers to engage in unobserved behavior or to abuse their position for self-economic payoffs. Corporate governance is therefore a way of ensuring that shareholder interests are correlated to managers.

A cursory perusal of the bank failures in the preceding chapter suggests that many causes of bank failures and distress relate to management actions and decisions which were not necessarily in the best interests of all other stakeholders. The review shows that managers enjoy significant freedom of action, due to the often lack of adequate control systems. This problem is exacerbated by the degree of shareholder dispersion. The agency problem that appears due to different risk preferences of the managers than the ones of other stakeholders can pose a systemic threat.

Despite having some criticisms based on simplistic assumptions in the complex business environment (Ross, 1973), incapability to offer standards concerning the opportunistic behavior demonstrated by managers; the agency theory offers 'a unique insight into information systems, outcome uncertainty, incentive and risk in corporate governance' (Eisenhardt, 1989).

SHAREHOLDERS AND MANAGERS CONFLICT OF INTERESTS

Ownership and control separation and different risk preferences of the main actors in an organization generate incentives for the agents to not act according to the principals. This is because it may not be in the agent's self-interest to pursue shareholder wealth maximization objective. The extent of shareholder dispersion determines their power, as power decreases with dispersion giving managers an opportunity to expropriate shareholders. The stability and riskiness of banking systems is affected by the existent ownership structure.

Dispersed shareholders imply little incentives to monitor managers. Excessive power by managers equals "the expropriation of dispersed shareholders by management" (Heremans, 2011). Shareholder dispersion also implies a lower level of power for the shareholders to obtain the necessary information to employ control. Shareholders in the banking sector find it more difficult to control managers because of the necessary knowledge of financial asymmetries and imperfections.

A review of the profiled bank failure cases in the introductory chapter of this book confirms the view by Jensen *et al.,* (1985) that the three main factors that generate conflict of interest at the management level are choice of effort, the differential risk exposure and differential time horizon. The agency theory addresses these problems through incentives and supervision. Supervision encompasses a critical watching and directing of activities or a course of action, that is overseeing an activity. The supervision mechanism is characterized by ex-post control and enters into the attribution of the board of directors. An incentive is anything that motivates or encourages someone to exert effort into doing an activity. The design of the compensation structure can also induce agents to act in the interest of shareholders. However, 'contracts offering incentives can give rise to dysfunctional behavior responses, where agents emphasize only those aspects of performance that are rewarded' (Pendergast, 1999). Consequently, conditional compensation has the potential to increase the level of risk-taking.

SHAREHOLDER THEORY

The shareholder theory was popularized by Friedman (1970). Friedman (1970) claimed that businesses "have only one social responsibility which is to use its resources to engage in activities designed to increase its profits in the context of the competition, legal and regulatory requirements". The shareholder theory is premised on the market economy principle which is a market-driven system that combines the private ownership of firms with intense competition in the pursuit of profit. The key market economy features are captured in the shareholder theory view: private ownership, competition and the profit motive. Profit maximization is the offspring of an economic system that is driven by price mechanism. The theory implies that individual entrepreneurs' profit maximization does maximize the overall society's economic welfare (Smith, 1776). However, this interpretation of shareholdership is sometimes lost and "the conventional model of the corporation, in both legal and managerial forms failed to discipline self-serving managerial behaviors" (Donaldson and Preston, 1995). The shareholder wealth maximization narrative has been reinforced by such influences as the globalization of capital markets, "a rise of institutional investors, increased shareholders activism and the growing importance of corporate governance" (Omran *et al.,* 2002).

The finance model or principal-agent theory underpins the shareholdership concept. This concept considers the maximization of shareholder wealth as the primary purpose of every enterprise because of the view that shareholders are the owners of firms and bear the highest risks (Sun, 2002). This view of the firm created the agency problem as managers push short-term policies that lead to their own interests against the shareholders' long-term profits objectives (Friedman, 1970; Jenson and Meckling, 1976). In addition, the myopic market model has the same claims as the shareholdership concept and adds the pursuit of short-term firm market value for the benefits of directors and management.

STAKEHOLDER THEORY

According to Wheeler *et al.,* (2002), the stakeholder theory was derived from a combination of sociological and organizational disciplines. The stakeholder theory contradicts the traditional economic theory which views the firm as shareholders' property. The theory was popularized by R. Edward Freeman (1984) in his seminal book *Strategic Management: A stakeholder Approach.* The book emphasized the importance of fully comprehending the dynamics of a business, and argues that a successful firm necessarily has to create value from its stakeholders. The success of a firm is measured by a wider approach which includes the full range of stakeholders. The purpose of the firm is defined by the overall value creation for stakeholders (Freeman, 1984). The stakeholder perspective is therefore the foremost fundamental perspective on performance. It is increasingly becoming essential for managers in organizations to consider the needs and wants of all their stakeholders.

The stakeholder theory incorporates philosophy, ethics, political theory, economics, law and organizational science. The theory is primarily concerned with the nature of stakeholder relationships in terms of both processes and outcomes for the firm and its stakeholders. The stakeholder view places responsibility to articulate business processes and to define and explain the relationship with stakeholders and how value will be created with the firm's management. The stakeholder view has been extended by several scholars to incorporate new areas. Donaldson and Preston (1995) present a framework based on three pillars – the normative, the instrumental, and the descriptive pillars. The normative branch revolves around the optimal guideline for a firm to manage its stakeholders, while the instrumental branch focuses on management results considering the interests of various stakeholders in governing the firm. The descriptive branch aims to observe and understand the interaction between managers and the firm's stakeholders.

The stakeholder theory views the firm as a nexus of explicit and implicit contracts and should therefore embrace all its stakeholders (Mintzberg, 1983; Freeman, 1984). An organization is viewed as a unique combination of various components which is worth more than the sum of its parts. It is the firm's responsibility to safeguard the interests of all who contribute to the general value creation. The theory is therefore a theoretical framework for analyzing the relationship between the company and the society. A firm cannot increase its value if it ignores the interests of its stakeholders. The theory recognizes that the corporation operates in a society and need resources from the planet and from the society. The corporation does not operate in isolation. Other models such as the Triple Bottom Line Reporting requirement and Carroll's Model of Organizational responsibilities take the stakeholder perspective of the firm. Corporations are artificial creations, *persona ficta*.

STEWARDSHIP THEORY

The system of capitalism should essentially be based on trust; trust that corporate leaders will be good stewards of the corporation's resources. The basis of the agency theory is the conflict or divergence of interests between the agent and the principal. The theory does not precisely explain whether or not anything causes their interests to be aligned.

The Stewardship Theory has its roots in sociology and psychology. The theory explains the relationship between managers and principals in which managers behave and act in the best interests of principals. A steward's behavior is "ordered such that pro-organizational, collectivistic behaviors have higher utility than individualistic self-serving behaviors" (Davis et al., 1997). According to empirical literature, below are the characteristics of stewards:

- Steward's behavior does not depart from the organization's interests
- A steward appreciates cooperation more than defection even if his/her interest are not aligned with the principal
- A steward does not substitute individualist behaviors for cooperative behaviors
- A steward seeks to achieve the objectives of the organization and thus, his/her behavior is collectivistic
- A steward's target is to protect shareholders' rights and maximize profits mainly through firm performance, because his/her utility functions will be maximized subsequently
- A steward's behavior can be regarded as organizationally centered

- An opportunity set of a steward is guided by the notion that the benefits obtained from pro-organizational, collectivistic behaviors are higher than that obtained from individualistic, self-serving behaviors
- A steward can be trusted due to his/her pro-organizational, collectivist behaviors
- A steward believes that his/her interests are aligned with the interests of the owner and thus, his/her motivation is oriented towards organizational objectives rather than personal needs

Donaldson (1997) suggested that "a steward protects and maximizes shareholders' wealth through firm performance, because by doing so, the steward's utility functions are maximized." Stewardship theory focuses on designing structures that empower and facilitate rather than control and monitor. The theory asserts that executives should be authorized to make decisions and act since they are not opportunistic agents. Employees are viewed as pro-organizational, trustworthy and collective-serving. Managers are therefore expected to integrate their goals as part of the organization. The agency theory views an employee as an economic being, thereby suppressing the individual aspirations of employees. The Stewardship theory on the other hand recognizes and offers maximum autonomy built on trust. The unification of the roles of the CEO and the Chairman is central to the Stewardship theory as a means to reduce agency costs and to have greater roles as stewards in the organization.

MANAGEMENT-HEGEMONY THEORY

The board of directors is viewed as a legal fiction dominated by management, that is, boards act as 'rubber stamp' with strategic decisions dominated by managers. Drucker (1981) stated that the board of directors is an impotent ceremonial and legal fiction. The Management-hegemony theory asserts that managers effectively control organizations and the role of the board is merely to approve the decisions taken by management.

Modern organizations are run by a class of professional managers. Organizational control is ceded to a new professional managerial class. Management-hegemony refers to the situation when the governing board of an organization serves simply as a 'rubber stamp' and all its strategic decisions are dominated and pre-empted by the professional managers. Organizations will inevitably resist board involvement in strategic decisions. Boards do not get involved in setting strategies.

NEW INSTITUTIONAL THEORY

The New Institutional Theory emphasizes the structure and composition of an organization's environment. The formal structure of organizations is not only a product of resource dependencies and technical demands, but is also influenced by institutional forces, including rational myths, knowledge legitimized through the educational system, public opinion, and the law.

Organizational practices and structures are considered as either reflections of, or responses to rules, beliefs and conventions built into the wider environment. The basis of the New Institutional Theory is founded on research done by John Meyer and Brian Rowan in the 1970s and 1980s on the effects of education on institutions. The theory's view on corporate governance highlights a dependence on legal and institutional frameworks, and successful corporate governance practices are thereby highly dependent on the institutional environment which the organization and respective stakeholders are embedded in.

ETHICS THEORY

The theory focuses on systemizing and recommending corporate governance concepts of right and wrong behavior. The Ethics Theory can be viewed from four broad categories: deontology, utilitarianism, rights and virtues. *Deontology* is important in ensuring consistency of results. *Utilitarianism* is based on one's ability to predict the consequences of an action. This is divided into Act utilitarianism and Rule utilitarianism. Act utilitarianism involves engaging in actions that benefit all stakeholders regardless of individual feelings and societal constraints. Rule utilitarianism is based on laws and ensuring fairness. The *rights* dimension of ethics focuses on what the society prescribes whilst the *virtue* ethical theory judges a person by his/her character rather than actions. It takes a person's morals, reputation and motivation into account. Virtue ethics focuses on moral excellence, goodness, chastity and good character. *Feminist ethics* theory emphasizes on empathy, healthy social relationships, loving care for each other and avoidance of harm. The discourse of ethics theory is concerned with peaceful settlement of conflicts. It is also referred to as augmentation ethics as it relies on establishing ethical truths by investigating the presuppositions of discourse.

CORPORATE GOVERNANCE CODES

This section reviews the nature of corporate governance codes in different economies. Reviewing the corporate governance codes is important in providing a comparative analysis of both the quality and effectiveness of national corporate governance legislation and the availability of proper corporate governance mechanisms and the weaknesses that should be tackled by organizations and legislators for improving the national corporate governance framework. The review of corporate governance codes in this section covers the following five key corporate governance areas that form part of the succeeding chapters of this book: (1) shareholder rights and activism, (2) board structure and roles, (3) risk management and internal controls, (4) transparency and disclosure of company information, and (5) stakeholder consideration. The economies reviewed in this section are aligned to the bank failure case studies profiled in the preceding chapter. The review of corporate governance covers Georgia and Germany.

CORPORATE GOVERNANCE CODE FOR BANKS - GEORGIA

Georgia is a country located at the intersection of Eastern Europe and Western Asia. Corporate governance legislation in Georgia is founded on the Law of Entrepreneurs, the Law on Activity of Commercial Banks, the Accounting and Auditing Law' and the Law on Securities Market. The National Bank of Georgia has issued various regulations related to corporate governance enhancement; for example, the Regulation on Fit and Proper Criteria for Administrators of Commercial Banks requires board members to have "university education in economics, audit, finance, banking, business administration, accounting or law. The appropriate qualification and professional experience, and the composition of the Supervisory board should ensure a variety of experience and skill-set, which corresponds to the scale and complexity of the bank's activities." The Association of Banks developed a corporate governance code for Commercial banks in 2009. The code is adopted under the 'comply or explain' mechanism in which banks should either comply with the proposed recommendations or explain the reasons for non-compliance. All companies in Georgia are organized under the two-tier board system. Supervisory boards in Georgia have an average of five (5) members.

Bank board members are required to "act reasonably and independently". The code for banks recommends banks to maintain an adequate balance between representatives of shareholders and independent board members. Independence according to the Code includes only negative "non-affiliation" requirements. Independent board members are expected to be "attentive to objectivity and impartiality regarding the rights of all shareholders and the supervision of executive management." The audit committee is established by decision of the supervisory board. This committee should be composed of independent members, that is, members not "connected to the bank and have no financial liability to the bank." The Code recommends that the audit committee should be made only of non-executive directors and includes at least one independent member of the board.

All companies in Georgia are required to include financial and non-financial information in their annual reports. Financial statements should be compiled in line with International Financial Reporting Standards (IFRS). The Code recommends that audit committees should develop policies and procedures related to external auditors rendering of non-audit services. All banks should have an internal audit function in place and a separate compliance function. There is no requirement to have a code of ethics in place. The right to appoint the external auditors is reserved to the general shareholders' meeting (GSM). Rotation of external auditor is not required. Related party transactions and conflict of interests are regulated.

Minority shareholders are entitled to call a general shareholders meeting and ask questions at the GSM. Shareholders are also entitled with pre-emptive rights in case of capital increase. Shareholders are also entitled to bring a derivative claim, but it depends on the approval of shareholders. Insider trading and self-dealing are regulated by law. Supermajority is required to approve major corporate decisions.

The corporate governance code of banks has no mandatory requirements and judicial practice on corporate governance issues is limited. The National Bank of Georgia is the supervisory authority and the regulator for the whole financial market in the country. It has the authority to address corporate governance failures and compel appropriate remedial action.

CORPORATE GOVERNANCE CODE FOR BANKS - GERMANY

The German corporate governance code presents statutory regulations for the governance of German listed companies. The Code contains internationally and nationally recognized standards for good corporate governance. The main focus of the code is to make the German corporate governance system transparent and understandable. The Code also aims to promote stakeholder trust in the management and supervision of listed German Stock Corporations. A dual board system is prescribed by law for German stock corporations. Shareholders have pre-emptive rights corresponding to their share of the equity capital, the shareholders meeting should be convened at least once a year. The Code promotes close cooperation between the management and the supervisory board. In the case of supervisory boards with co-determination, representatives of the shareholders and of the employees should prepare the supervisory board separately. Enterprises employing over 500 or 2000 employees should ensure that the employees are represented in the supervisory board through one-third or one-half representation respectively.

The management board is mandated to inform the supervisory board regularly, without delay and comprehensively of all issues important to the enterprise with regard to strategy, planning, business development, risk situation, risk management and compliance. If members of the management and supervisory boards violate the duty of care and diligence of a prudent and conscientious member, they are liable to the company for damages. Connected lending transactions should be approved by the supervisory board. The management and supervisory boards report each year on corporate governance and publish the corporate governance report in connection with the statement on corporate governance.

The respective total compensation of the individual management and board member is determined by the full supervisory board. The total compensation is determined in plenary session based on a performance assessment. The following criteria determines appropriate compensation, tasks of the individual member, his/her personal performance, the economic situation, the performance and outlook of the enterprise as well as the common level of compensation taking into account the peer companies and compensation structure in place in other areas of the company. The Code emphasizes that the compensation structure must be oriented toward sustainable growth of the enterprise. A compensation report must be prepared as part of the management report outlining the compensation system for management board members.

The Code recommends that companies treat all shareholders in the same way as regards information access. The external auditor should be commissioned by the supervisory board including concluding on the audit fees. The auditor should report without delay on all facts and events of importance for the task of the supervisory board which arise during the performance audit.

CORPORATE GOVERNANCE CODE FOR BANKS - ZIMBABWE

Zimbabwe launched an all-embracing code on corporate governance (ZIMCODE). The Code purportedly contains international best practices and standards on corporate governance and gives the business community a platform to responsibly conduct business. The Code highlights institutional failures within the banking sector, owner management conflicts, corporate power concentration, corporate scandals and corporate failures, and the emergence and growth of unethical corporate leadership as the driving forces to the adoption of the national code. However, Section 2 of the code states that "special sectors such as banking and financial services sector, partnerships, trusts and small to medium enterprises should have specific codes of their own which take a sector approach to corporate governance".

The Zimbabwean banking sector, guided by a code of ethics on disclosure of information, is one of the most secretive and largely opaque business landscape where every piece of information is insulated under the "confidentiality" ambit. Any information released can be a source of business risk. All corporate activities in Zimbabwe are mainly regulated by the Companies Act (Chapter 24:03) and Zimbabwe Stock Exchange Act (Chapter 24:18), and Public Finance Management Act (Chapter 22:19). The Institute of Directors of Zimbabwe (IoDZ) also plays an important role in developing and enforcing rules and corporate governance standards and governing corporate conduct with reference to the Cadbury Report and the King Report. The listing rules adopted by The ZSE are based on the London Stock Exchange (LSE) and the Johannesburg Stock Exchange (JSE). Prior to the launch of the ZIMCODE, The King II Code has been adopted by most parastatals in Zimbabwe. Most private sector institutions developed their own in-house corporate governance manuals.

As shown in the Table below, Zimbabwe has numerous legislations that govern corporate activities. These legislations are essential in the determination of the corporate governance model in Zimbabwe. Organizations that comply with these legislations are likely to have an enhanced level of organizational effectiveness.

Legislations governing corporations in Zimbabwe

Prevention of Corruption Act, Chapter 9:16	Audit and Exchequer Act, Chapter 22:03
Postal and Telecommunications Services Act, Chapter 12:02	Public Accountants and Auditors Act, Chapter 27:03
Criminal Procedure and Evidence Act, Chapter 9:07	Bank Use Promotion and Suppression of Money Laundering Act, Chapter 24:24
Exchange Control Act, Chapter 22:05	Serious Offences Act, Chapter 9:17
Companies Act, Chapter 24:03	Building Societies Act, Chapter 24:02
Sales Tax Act, Chapter 23:08	Public Finance Management Act, Chapter 22:19
Banking Act, Chapter 24:01	Reserve Bank Act, Chapter 22:15

It is essential to understand that corporate governance codes and laws alone cannot address fully the deeper issues in corporate governance deficiencies. It is impossible to legislate behavioral issues and sound corporate governance.

GUIDING CORPORATE GOVERNANCE FRAMEWORKS

The development of panoply of sound corporate governance principles and practices enshrined in legislation or through other regulatory mechanisms is being done at all levels, that is, at national, regional and international level (Abdullah and Valentine, 2009). The most significant corporate governance initiatives at international level are: OECD Corporate Governance Standards, Basel Committee Core Principles, and Basel Committee work on corporate governance. In the United Kingdom (UK), the rising corporate scandals in the 1980s and 1990 led to a growing distrust of, and skepticism towards managers and directors in organizations (Smith, 2010). Increasing irregularities in financial disclosure necessitated the establishment of the Financial Aspects of Corporate Governance Committee resulting in the Cadbury Report in 1992. *The Cadbury Report* encompasses a Code of Best Practice and its recommendations were incorporated into the London Stock Exchange (LSE) listing rules. The Cadbury Report was followed by the *Rutterman Report* in 1994, which focused on reporting the effectiveness of a company's internal control systems.

In 1995 the *Greenbury Report* was established and it recommended extensive disclosure of directors' remuneration in annual reports. It also recommended the establishment of a remuneration committee comprised of non-executive directors. The Hampel Committee followed the Greenbury Report and was established to assess the implementation of the Cadbury and Greenbury Reports. The *Hampel Report* led to the Combined Code of Corporate Governance (1998) covering such areas as board structure and operations, directors' remuneration, accountability and audit, relations with institutional shareholders, and institutional shareholders' responsibilities. These reports offer essential principles and practices of corporate governance and are useful in assessing the effectiveness of the corporate governance of individual institutions. The Combined Code of Corporate Governance is regarded as an international benchmark for sound corporate governance.

Corporate performance is also affected by the implementation of the combined code of corporate governance. The Combined Code of Corporate Governance offers companies to comply with its principles or explain reasons for non-compliance. Under the Combined Codes of 1998 and 2003, companies are required to report in their annual report how they will have applied the Code Principle and Code Provisions relating to internal control. This is essential in driving inclusive organizational effectiveness. The Turnbull Committee was established in 1998 to provide guidance to companies, resulting in the 1999 *Turnbull Guidance*, "Internal Control: Guidance for Directors on the Combined Code". The Securities and Exchange Commission (SEC) approved the Guidance as framework for management report the adequacy of internal control structures and overall financial reporting procedures in compliance with the *Sarbanes-Oxley Act (SOX)*. The SOX is a United States (US) federal law which was introduced in 2002 following the Enron scandal in 2001 and the dissolution of Arthur Andersen. The Act was established to expand financial reporting reliability for public companies through regulations to ensure audit firms become more accountable by being more objective and independent of their clients.

During the period 2001 to 2009 several reviews were made including: Myners Review (2001), Directors Remuneration and Report Guidelines (2002), and Higgs Report (2003). Corporate governance in the UK is also significantly determined by the European Union policies and practices. The European Commission's "Corporate Governance and Company Law Action Plan" (2003) proposed a mix of legislative and regulatory measures which would affect all member States relating to: "disclosure requirements; exercise of voting rights; disclosure by institutional investors; and responsibilities of board members". The Global Financial Crisis 2008/09 has cast a shadow over the western governance model (Yip, 2013). *The Turner Review (2009)* was a UK regulatory response to the global banking crisis. The Turner Review outlines recommendations on the redesign of regulation and supervisory approach in order to create a more solvent and stable banking system. It also focuses on improving the effectiveness of internal risk management and corporate governance. In response to the experience of critical loss and failure in the banking systems, *The Walker Review (2009)* was published. This review focuses on examining UK banking industry corporate governance and makes recommendations on:

- UK banking institutions' risk management effectiveness at board level;
- the competencies and independence required on the boards of UK banking institutions;
- the effectiveness of board practices and the performance of corporate governance committees such as audit, risk, remuneration and nomination;
- institutional shareholders' role in engaging effectively with companies and monitoring boards; and
- compliance of the UK corporate governance frameworks with international best practice.

The adoption of these recommendations is essential in driving organizational effectiveness through the implementation of effective risk management practices, enhancing the performance of directors, improve overall board effectiveness, and ensuring compliance with international best practices (The Walker Review, 2009). The focus of the Walker Review recommendations is therefore to improve organizational effectiveness at institutional, industry, and inclusive level.

Literature acknowledges that there is no universally accepted global set of principles that are applicable to board structures (Raeze, 2009). The existent corporate governance principles are merely guidelines rather than universal rules of corporate governance (Gul and Tsui, 2004). Corporate governance is concerned with "the establishment of an appropriate legal, economic and institutional environment that facilitate the growth and sustainability of organizations for maximizing shareholder value while being conscious of and providing for the wellbeing of the wider stakeholders" (Kenya Private Sector Initiative for Corporate Governance, 2000). Below are the four key corporate governance issues according to The Basel Committee (2006):

- the appropriate involvement of the board in developing and approving the bank's strategy;
- setting and enforcing clear lines of responsibility throughout the organization;
- instituting compensation policies which are consistent with the bank's overall strategic intent; and
- adequately managing operational risks that lack transparency.

CHAPTER 2

SHAREHOLDERS AND CORPORATE GOVERNANCE

Shareholders are regarded as the owners of corporations; however, they often do not run them. Despite shareholders not being involved in how firms are managed and directed, they are central to corporate governance. From a legal perspective, shareholders do not own the corporation – they own securities that give them a less-than well-defined claim on its earnings. In Law and in practice, shareholders do not have the final say over most big corporate decisions – boards of directors do. The shareholders elect directors, who then appoint professional managers, who in turn run corporations. A shareholder is a person or entity who buys and holds shares in a company having a share capital. This chapter discusses the types, roles, incentives, interests and powers of shareholders in corporate governance.

TYPES OF SHAREHOLDERS

Shareholders are distinguished as minority and majority shareholders, comprising controlling blockholders and institutional investors. Shareholders can either be large or small shareholders. Small shareholders are individuals and/or entities whose holdings are small in absolute terms and relative to the company's total outstanding shares, and is often a small part of the investors' total portfolio. This category of shareholders has little power in terms of controlling the board of directors due to the smallness of their shareholding. Small shareholders also have little motivation to control the corporation due to the small personal portfolios invested in the corporation. The small shareholders are important to corporate governance because they can be a source of conflict if the organization fails to properly integrate them in decision making and corporate governance.

Large shareholders own a significant stake of voting shares in the corporation to justify their active role in monitoring directors and management. These can either be controlling shareholders or institutional investors. There are instances where large institutional investors can be just as passive as small shareholders. In such instances, their main interest could be to achieve favorable investment results, and they might have little appetite for corporate management and corporate governance. Large shareholders can cause corporate governance challenges if they adopt a domineering behavior that compromise corporate decisions.

Controlling shareholders are those with enough shares under their control to dominate or strongly influence the board of directors and to choose management. Controlling shareholders are a solution to the agency problem that arises from the separation of ownership and control in public corporations.

Shareholders influence the policies of a firm through electing directors, voting on changes to the corporate structure or charter, or through proxy contests and shareholder proposals. Shareholders also determine the vision of the firm and communicate the vision to the board of directors. Shareholders play a relatively minor role in the governance process of companies, as their remedial rights are generally reactive as opposed to providing board of directors with a meaningful opportunity to participate in the strategic planning and decision-making process of the company. The UK Companies Act 2006, indicate that shareholders are involved in the approval of major corporate decisions. These involve corporate decisions that have the capacity to affect shareholders' rights. Examples of fundamental corporate matters that should be made and approved by shareholders are removal of a director from office, mergers & acquisitions transactions, sale of company assets, and changing the company name or authorizing service contracts from a director.

The shareholders are mandated to attend the general shareholder meetings and discuss issues raised on the agenda. As covered in Chapter 11, the general shareholder meetings provide a platform for shareholders to exercise their voting rights, which is a mode of decision-taking by a plurality of people. Voting rights complement and compensate shareholders for incomplete contracts (Baums, 2000), and thus, constitute an important part of the share value (Amzaleg *et al.*, 2005).

The Canadian Business Corporations Act (CBCA) identifies the fundamental matters that require shareholder approval as: effecting corporate amalgamations or reorganizations; disposal of corporate assets or disinvestments; changing the corporation's share capital; confirming by-laws; and changing the board composition or size. Shareholders also play a stewardship role of the corporation, make financial investments, and elect directors and supervise management.

LEGAL RIGHTS OF SHAREHOLDERS

- To receive dividends, if declared by the board of directors
- To vote on:
  - ✓ Members of the board
  - ✓ Major mergers and acquisitions
  - ✓ Charter and bylaw changes
  - ✓ Proposals by stakeholders
- To receive annual reports on the company's financial performance and condition
- To sell their own shares of stocks to others

- Pre-emptive right, that is, the right to acquire additional shares prior to share being available for purchase by the general public.

SHAREHOLDER ACTIVISM

Shareholder activism implies, shareholders, taking an active role in a company. It is the way in which shareholders assert their power as the *de facto* owners of the company. Shareholder activism refers to the active influence on firm policy and practices through the use of ownership position (Sjostrom, 2008). Through shareholder activism, shareholders can exercise and enforce their rights to enhance long-term shareholder value (Low, 2004). Shareholder activism refers to strategic actions taken by shareholders with the explicit intention of influencing corporation's policies and practices, rather than as latent intentions implicit in ownership stakes or trading behavior. Shareholder activism takes many forms: attending annual shareholder meetings (AGM) and other shareholder meetings to ask directors to account for various issues, vote on directors' remuneration and remuneration policy, engaging management and directors on contentious issues; raise audit concerns, questioning board composition and engineering the removal of unsuitable directors. These shareholder responsibilities are crucial to organizational effectiveness.

According to Armour and Cheffins (2010), activism can either be *"defensive"* or *"offensive"*. Defensive activism occurs when shareholders (e.g pension funds and mutual funds) become dissatisfied with corporate performance or corporate governance practices and thus react by lobbying for relevant changes. This type of shareholder activism is defensive in the sense that activist seek to protect pre-existing investments. Offensive activism occurs when investors lacking a substantial stake in a company, build-up their holdings offensively on the assumption that organizational changes will overcome failures and, thus maximize shareholder returns. Shareholders can also exercise their activism through either the *"voice"* or *"exit"* approach. This means shareholders unhappy about firm performance will invest effort and patience into the company (voice) and not the option of transferring shares (exit) (Hirshmann, 1978).

Shareholder activism follows evolutionary patterns (Graves *et al.,* 2009). Corporate matters can follow different paths over time. The pattern depends on the shifting regulatory environment or on a myriad of factors internal and external to the company. The motivation behind shareholder activism can be financially driven or socially driven (Judge *et al.,* 2010). Financially driven activism focuses on the financial performance of companies and seeks to pressure management for an improved portfolio performance. These activists can be entrepreneurial, e.g asset management groups, hedge funds, private equity funds and venture capital funds that are differentiated by their investment strategies. Individual investors also fall under this financially-driven activist's category. This stream of activists embraces the shareholder primacy view of the firm and as such adopts executionary approaches to maximize shareholder wealth. It treats activism that deviates from concerns with shareholder value or governance as irrelevant or frivolous (Thomas and Cotter, 2007). It is therefore executionary as it focuses merely on economic outcomes or specific targets as determined by the shareholders.

Socially driven activist focuses on economic equity issues and seeks more justice in society particularly when the latter aligns with the financial interests of the activist. These activists include the shareholder community or non-profit groups including religious, environmental, labor organizations, and interest groups that pursue social issues for the principle-based purposes. This stream of activists is stakeholder centered as shareholder activists raises social issues in annual shareholder meetings and corporate boardrooms.

Below is a review of shareholder activism in Canada, Zimbabwe and Georgia.

SHAREHOLDER ACTIVISM – CANADA

Canadian corporations are adopting proactive business models due to the increased and continual exposure to sophisticated shareholder activism. Corporate Canada has witnessed increased proxy contests due to the emergence of tactical economic players in the early 2000s. Shareholders in Canada have the ability to vote for individual directors rather than voting on a single slate. In the event that shareholder activists and the corporation fails to agree on a case, numerous legal tools are available to shareholders under Canadian laws that allow activists to take their case directly to all shareholders or even replace the board of the corporation with activist nominees. Shareholder proposals, shareholder-requisitioned meetings, and proxy battles to replace a sitting board are deceptively easy to initiate under Canadian law. Voting for directors at most Canadian corporations is currently based on a plurality system, whereby shareholders cannot vote against directors at director elections. Rather, shareholders are only entitled to vote "for" or "withhold" their vote for director nominees. In a plurality system, "withhold" votes not count, and where the number of directors nominated for election equals the number of available seats on the board, a director could technically be elected with only one "for" vote which could come from the director himself.

Corporate and securities laws in Canada allow directors to be nominated and voted on as a slate, and where slate ballots are used, the only option available to shareholders is to vote "for" or "withhold" on the entire slate of director nominees, with no opportunity to vote on directors individually.

SHAREHOLDER ACTIVISM – ZIMBABWE

The Zimbabwe Corporate Governance Code (ZIMCODE) addresses the issue of corporate control. The control of the corporation is based on the fact that shareholders provide the risk capital which is managed by the board. Shareholders in Zimbabwe have the right exercise their voting rights at the Annual General Meeting (AGM) and influence the direction of the company. The exercise of shareholders' rights is guided by the company statutes such as company constitutions. These include share certificates, memorandum of association and articles of association. The corporate governance responsibilities of shareholders include reviewing the performance of the board and holding the board to account.

SHAREHOLDER ACTIVISM – GEORGIA

The Supervisory and Management Board should ensure effective and fair relations with shareholders. These boards should ensure that as many shareholders as possible participate at the general meeting of shareholders. The shareholders exercise their rights at the general meeting of shareholders, and there should be equitable treatment of all shareholders. Minority shareholders are entitled to call a general shareholders meeting (GSM) and ask questions at the GSM. The shareholders should have access to information from members of the Supervisory and Management Board.

CHAPTER 3

THE BOARD OF DIRECTORS

"A small body of determined spirits fired up by an unquenchable faith in their mission can alter the course of history" - Mahatma Gandhi

A board is reckoned as a team brought together to work towards achieving organizational goals. Board of directors is a collective of people who are nominated by the shareholders of a company and responsible for making decisions on their behalf as it would be impossible for the shareholders to meet frequently to make detailed decisions, especially when the company has a larger number of shareholders (Yung, 2009). The board of directors is a pivot between management team and shareholders. Its mission is to link between the vast number of shareholders dispersed around the world and the main managers. The difference between the board of directors and other teams in an organization is that the board is not in the organization's chain of command whilst such teams as executives, managers and staff are in the chain of command. The board provides technical assistance to the executive and management teams.

AN OVERVIEW OF THE BOARD FUNCTIONS

There is a clear difference between the main responsibilities of board of directors and managers. In the book, *Corporate Governance and Chairmanship: A Personal View*, Sir Adrian Cadbury distinguishes between direction and management: "it is the job of the board to set the ends – that is to say, to define what the company is in business for – and it is the job of the executive to decide the means by which the ends are best achieved. They must do so, however, within rules of conduct and limits of risk that has been set by the board. The board is ultimately accountable for both the company's purpose and for the means of achieving it. The task, however, for which the board alone is responsible, is the determination of corporate ends."

Boards have a crucial role towards strategy and organizational effectiveness. These two roles are critical to sound corporate governance in the banking sector considering today's highly volatile business operating environment. The 1987 Mintzberg's 5Ps indicates the different characteristics of strategy as briefly highlighted below:

- Plan – an intended direction and course of action
- Ploy – a maneuver to outwit competitors.
- Pattern – a consistent pattern of past behavior. These include strategies that have been implemented before.
- Position – how to position brands, products or the company. It determines the company's position in the market.
- Perspective – the determination of the board in terms of finding out how different stakeholders perceive the organization.

Organizational effectiveness represents the outcome of organizational activities over a period of time. There are different conceptions of organizational effectiveness including profitability, financial-market, multi-stakeholder satisfaction and quality of firm's transformations. The evolution of organizational effectiveness comprises the five models explained below:

Model	Explanation
Goal Model	This model is the most common theoretical perspective on effectiveness. The conventional organizational effectiveness model relies on the firm's vision as a rational set of arrangements focused on achieving set goals (Goodman *et al.,* 1977). The model posits that organizations can be understood as rational entities. The primary focus of the rational goal model is the ability of an organization to achieve predefined goals. The

	accomplishment of outcomes is the basic measure of effectiveness (Etzioni 1960). "Its focus is on the output, to figure out the essential operating objectives like profit, innovation and finally product quality" (Schermerhorn *et al.,* 2004).
Systems Model	The system model emphasizes the means towards the accomplishment of specific ends. The focus is on inputs, resources and processes (Yuchtman and Seashore, 1967). Effectiveness is explained in terms of the ability to obtain necessary resources from the environments outside the organization (Schermerhorn *et al.,* 2004). The conception of the organization is grounded in the open system approach whereby the inputs, transformation process and outputs are considered part of whole and not independent components. The model analyzes the ability of managers and directors to efficiently distribute resources among various subsystems' needs. The organization, in this case, is defined as a network of interrelated subsystems.
Strategic Constituencies	The goal and systems model are expanded under the strategic constituencies model. The model adds the expectations of all the powerful stakeholders of the organization (Connolly, Colon and Deutch, 1980). The effects of the organization on its key stakeholders are addressed by the strategic constituencies model (Schermerhorn *et al.,* 2004). Effectiveness is therefore a measure of the minimal satisfaction of all stakeholders (strategic constituencies). The strategic constituencies have different roles in an organization. Examples of such roles include consumers of the products or services,

	resource providers, facilitators of the organization's output, and dependents of the organization (Cameron, 1981). An organization is therefore perceived as a set of internal and external constituencies that negotiate a complex set of constraints, goals and referents (Goodman *et al.*, 1977).
Competing Values	This model constitutes a synthesis and an extension of the goal, system and strategic-constituencies models (Quinn and Rohrbaugh, 1983). Effectiveness under this model is perceived as an exercise grounded in values. Organizational values therefore forms the foundation of this model, hence three sets of competing values are juxtaposed to form different definitions of effectiveness. These sets of values are: (i) means-ends dilemma, (ii) the internal-external focus dilemma, and (iii) the control-flexibility dilemma.
Ineffectiveness Model	The focus of this model is on the factors that inhibit successful organizational performance. An organization is therefore perceived as a set of problems and faults (Cameron, 1984). Its basic assumption is that "it is easier, more accurate, more consensual and more beneficial to identify problems and faults (ineffectiveness) than criteria of competencies (effectiveness)". Organizational effectiveness is therefore defined as the absence of inhibiting factors

In reviewing and assessing board effectiveness, boards can adopt any of the following three different stances:

- *Exclusionary stance* – model as a single best approach. This methodological monism stance involves reliance on only a single model of evaluation.
- *Cumulative stance* – the cumulative stance considers models as building blocks in a mapped domain. This stance focuses on the interconnected of different models in line with the sequence of tasks or activities. In view of complexity science and Systems Thinking, the cumulative evaluation stance should be supported by process mapping and modelling methodologies.
- *Complementary stance* – based on the system thinking perspective, the complementary stance indicates that each model complements another. The decision engineering methodologies are essential in this regard. The cumulative and complementary stance considers methodological pluralism approach as central to the review and assessment of board effectiveness.

The review of board effectiveness should strive to deliberately avoid the methodological monism stance, that is, the insistence on using a single evaluation or assessment method. "Methodological monism doctrine implicitly or explicitly states the unity of epistemology in all disciplines" (Tamas, 2008). Based on the complexity of organizations, it is essential for the board review process to adopt the methodological pluralism (cumulative and complementary stance) in order to ensure integrative and structured results. Methodological pluralism accepts the aprioristic introduction of methodological thoughts from other sources of knowledge (Tamas, 2008), or from other complementary methods of inquiry. From an action research perspective, methodological pluralism perspective suggests that every phenomenon has its own subject-dependent methodology. The study sub-disciplines have their own specific methodologies; therefore, the inquiry into the effectiveness of the board can be undertaken with the help of many suitable methodologies.

Boards are essential for strategic decision-making and monitoring strategy implementation. It is the board's responsibility to regularly monitor the performance of management and the overall performance of the firm. The board performs fiduciary duties, such as the duty of care and monitoring the management activities with a view to minimize or eliminate compliance risk. The two main functions of the board are those of advising and monitoring (Raheya, 2015). Directors use the board meetings as a forum to develop the mission of the organization, establishing and reviewing the firm's mission and for implementation of strategic initiatives to meet the firm's objectives. The board is also greatly involved in strategic thinking and strategic leadership. Boards champion organizational transformation, challenge the organization's basic assumptions and help to foster a culture of exploitation and experimentation in a volatile, uncertain, complex and ambiguous operating environment.

The board is also involved in monitoring the market in order to keep abreast of performance, examining management proposals, and specifying strategic option to management. Based on the principles of Fitness Landscape Theory, market monitoring involves reviewing the external environmental factors and the industry specific factors in order to ensure fitness. "The board functions include establishing strategic direction, overseeing the firm's strategy, assessing and monitoring performance" (Tricker, 1984). The board's main duty is to protect and promote the interests of the shareholders (Rossouw *et al.,* 2002). In view of leadership theory, the five practices of leadership as developed by Kouzes and Posner should be displayed by all members of the board of directors: model the way, inspire a shared vision, challenge the process, enable others to act, and encourage the heart. According to extant literature, some of the board functions are steward of the enterprise, model of values and core values, guardian of strong governance, strategist, risk and scenario planner, public face and market maker, custodian of capital markets, and global advocate (Renjen, 2012; Kemp, 2006; Vafeas, 1999).

The board also plays a role of guaranteeing conformance and ensuring the performance of management in the firm. The board performs these roles through different functions such as executive action (strategy), direction (advice), service and resource support (resource dependence, supervision (monitoring and accountability) (Brenna, 2006). The integration of corporate governance conformance and performance is referred to as Enterprise Governance. Boards therefore point organizations in the right direction through providing counsel during strategy formulation, roll-out and on-going adaptation to market developments. Boards also help to define and champion an organization's identity.

In dynamic organizations, boards help management to develop and refine corporate strategy. In order to refine the corporate strategy, the board engages in dialogue with management to confirm that strategy aligns with the vision, mission and core values of the organization. In view of the rapidly changing business environment and the widespread digital complexities, boards can help management examine the triggers that might propel the organization and its marketplace beyond the new normal. Boards can also explore for promising adjacencies to their current core business. This demands that the board leverage on information technology and understands what nascent Artificial Intelligence (AI) applications might bring to their company. In directing the organization, the board should have a broader perspective of organizational growth. This is because organizational growth does not simply imply enlargement. Rather, it also embraces development, refinement, adaptation, as well as change management. The board should be concerned with cherishing and nurturing the vision for the organization and maintaining strategic oversight of the entity. The board is also involved in finding out, appointing and firing the CEO.

Empirical studies summarized the main role of the board in agency control, strategic decision and policy support role (McNulty and Pettigrew, 1999), to provide a network of firm reputation (Finkelstein and Hambrick, 1996) and the resource acquirer role

(Johnson *et al.,* 1996). The primary board responsibilities can be summarized   as: (1) strategy, leadership, controlling, management and reporting (Cadbury, 1992; OECD, 2004); (2) shareholder advocate (Shleifer and Vishny, 1996; Macey, 2008; Monks, 2001); (3) directing, controlling and reporting (Nicholson and Kiel, 2007; Aguillera, 2005); (4) monitoring, serving management, strategy, resource provision (Ong and Wan, 2008).

THE MULTIPLE ROLES OF CORPORATE EXECUTIVES

Corporate executives support the board of directors and directly engage the board on most corporate matters. The corporate executives are part of the chain of command and oversee the performance of managers. Highlighted below are some of the multiple roles of corporate executives.

- *Identity creating role* – organizations need to develop distinct identity and in view of the intensity of competition, uniqueness characterize identity.
- *Enabling role* – facilitate the development of resources. This involves creating an environment which stimulate people to contribute their maximum.
- *Synergizing role* – multiplying all resources. Maximize utilization so that results outweigh the sum-total of all the resources.
- *Balancing role* - conformity and creativity balance. When conformity goes beyond a point, it does not contribute to organizational growth. Stabilization of the process and innovation because unless the organization stabilizes its main process it cannot effectively achieve the results. Without innovation it may not be able to move in new directions and respond to new challenges and pressures.
- *Linkage building role* – foster linkages between the organization and the environment. This is facilitated through dialogue between executives and all stakeholders.

36

- *Futuristic role* – ability to peep into the future. This role requires discovery and predictive methodologies and skills among directors, executives and managers.
- *Making impact* – influencing other institutions and the environment. The executives should operate with a broader perspective regarding people, planet and profit.
- *Providing super-ordination* – give a sense of fulfillment to members. Super-ordination, that is, a feeling that one is working for a higher goal which cannot be achieved single-handedly and for which collaborative work is necessary and provides higher motivation and satisfaction to people.

SKILLS AND QUALIFICATIONS OF BOARD MEMBERS

The skills of board members are primarily centered on strategic thinking and strategic leadership. The board is undoubtedly the critical asset for every organization (Homan and Renz, 1997). The need for governing boards, particularly in banking; to be informed, engaged and effective has never been greater due to the disruptive pace of digitization and intensity of competition in the banking space. Increasing competition for resources, greater organizational complexities and sophistication and potential of external regulations drive the need for high quality boards that possess Organization Development (OD) skills. Boards are expected to be aware of and responsible for complying with regulations. Board members need to ask senior executives and management to demonstrate compliance with laws and regulations. As discussed in the previous section, board members are responsible for setting policy and providing oversight to ensure that the resources that are entrusted to the organization are used for the purposes intended. A board that understands its roles and responsibilities provides the fiduciary oversight required for the success of the organization.

Board members should possess leadership skills because the directors guide and direct others and help to move the organization toward common, agreed upon goals. Leadership can be defined by both a set of traits and a set of behavior.

LEADERSHIP TRAITS FOR BOARD MEMBERS

- *Mission focused* – constantly bringing discussions and decision-making to the fundamental reason, that is, the *raison detre*.
- *Visionary* – ability to see beyond the current situation. Imagine alternate futures and scenarios for the organization.
- *Analytical* – weighs options, risks and benefits of decisions and is able to lay out the rationale for reaching a particular decision.
- *Objective* – invite and consider multiple options and entertain various viewpoints when considering decisions.

LEADERSHIP BEHAVIORS FOR BOARD MEMBERS

- *Are dependable* – the degree to which members follow through with commitment and do what they say they will.
- *Are honest* – the degree of integrity and trustworthy of the member. This is a measure of the member's commitment to the fiduciary responsibilities.
- *Are engaged* – prepared, ready for discussions and able to make decisions and stand by them.
- *Are effective communicators* – provide information and opinions in a respectful, non-judgmental fashion that allows others to easily hear and understand their viewpoints.
- *Are courageous* – willing to have difficult discussions with other members about the organization and its performance, putting the ultimate success of the organization before desires to avoid conflict or unpleasant conversations.

The vowels of strategy below explain the essential behaviors that board members should have in order to drive organizational effectiveness. These vowels are adapted from Justine

Chinoperekweyi's unpublished Ph.D., Thesis on Corporate Governance.

Behaviour	Explanation
Aspire to a vision	This involves the commitment to the organization's vision and the active monitoring of the CEO and executive team members.
Evaluate	This involves conscious efforts to understand the business environment, and being entrepreneurial.
Integrate	Encompasses the integration of all business units and a commitment to implementation of plans.
Optimize and Oversee	The board and CEO should have a sense of ownership and oversee the operations of the business
Uphold	This encompasses the board and CEO commitment to duty of care, honesty, candor, and loyalty.

Good board members exhibit passion, commitment and vision and they articulate these clearly. They have the ability to communicate with and engage others. Resource-dependence theory suggests that organizations must acquire the resources necessary for effective performance (Pfeffer and Solancik, 1978). Within the service-based and knowledge-based industry, one of the most important resources is capable, talented and committed individuals. Hillman and Dalziel (2003) recognize that board members are an instrumental link to capture resources for organizations. Obtaining competent and capable board members is vital because they can bring key resources such as knowledge, skills, relationships and money that strengthen the organization thereby enhancing its capacity to thrive and win.

Studies on board performance have identified the board performance Key Performance Indicators (KPIs) as meeting attendance, the quality of that attendance (whether the member comes prepared), constructive contribution to conversations and the business of the board, and the necessary knowledge and skills to perform the role. This last feature is reinforced in the work of Hillman and Dalziel (2003), who introduced a concept called *"board capital"*, which they explain as capital that consists of both human capital (experience, expertise and reputation) and relational capital (network of ties to other firms and external contingencies)." Research supports the fact that boards high in board capital are more inclined to provide necessary advice and counsel (Westphal, 1998), improve organizational legitimacy and external constituencies (Hillman *et al.,* 1999), and improve the ability to organizations to acquire necessary resources (Provan, 1980). These elements are essential in driving organizational effectiveness and as such should be intertwined with the methods of optimal solutions in order to ensure sustainability.

BOARD QUALIFICATION

- High financial literacy
- Extensive knowledge of the company's business and industry
- Risk oversight and management expertise
- Leadership experience – this is important to provide the company with unique insights. It gives the ability to identify and develop those qualities in others. Demonstrate a practical understanding of organizations, processes, strategy and risk management, and know how to drive change and growth.
- Technological experience – the success of any modern organization depends on developing and investing in new technologies and access to new ideas.
- Global experience – the understanding of global business operations help to identify opportunities and manage risks associated with globalization.
- Legal expertise – this is essential in managing compliance risk that result from the dynamic legal environment.

BOARD DUTIES

The following are some of the duties of board members in an organization.

- Duty to inform – ensuring that all relevant information about the corporation is released to the public
- Loyalty – fulfill all fiduciary duties towards all stakeholders and corporation as a whole
- Duty of care – this involves the duty to effectively use the organization to generate revenue.
- Duty to be objective and independently minded

TYPES OF BOARDS OR BOARD STRUCTURE

It is important to understand the definitions used to describe directors and the boards. Board structure, which is concerned with the balance of power, affiliations and positions of members, is a foundation for an effective board and is at the heart of board performance and accountability (Tricker, 1994). As discussed earlier, directors can either be non-executive, executive, or independent directors. An executive director is also an executive of the company, such as a CEO or CFO being in the full-time salaried employment of the company. A non-executive director is not part of the management and is valued for external perspectives and unique expertise. Independent in ordinary parlance means vary, but usually require the person to be free of financial, family and employment ties, or any other meaningful relation with the company, its directors and employees. The King III defined the independent director based on the following seven characteristics:

- Is not a representative of a shareholder who has the ability to control or significantly influence management or the board
- Does not have direct or indirect interests in the company
- Has not been employed by the company or the group of which it currently forms part in any executive capacity

41

- Is not a member of the immediate family of an individual who is, or has during the preceding three financial years, been employed by the company or the group in any executive capacity
- Is not a professional advisor to the company or the group
- Is free from any business or other relationships which could be seen by an objective outsider to interfere materially with the individual's capacity to act in an independent manner
- Does not receive remuneration contingent upon the performance of the company.

Boards can be either one-tier or two-tier. A one-tier board or unitary board delegates day-to-day business activities to the CEO, management team, or executive committee, and is composed of both executive and non-executive members. Leadership is in the hands of the Chairman, who may also be CEO of the company.

A two-tier board, or dual board divides supervisory and management duties into two separate bodies. The Supervisory Board oversees the Management Board, which handles day-to-day operations. The one-tier system is found in countries with common law traditions whilst the dual system is common in countries with civil law traditions. The supervisory board consists of non-executive directors and is mainly concerned with supervision. The Supervisory Board oversees management, appoints and dismisses members of the Management Board and approves financial accounts. It is also responsible for networking with stakeholders (Jungmann, 2006). The Chairman preside the Supervisory Board and must be a person different from the CEO. Two-tier boards allow for a greater opportunity for stakeholder inclusion than the one-tier boards (Solomon, 2013).

Many boards operate as "hybrids", but here are the main kinds of boards:

- *Advisory board* – provide advice, counsel or study a situation and make recommendations for action. These boards typically have no legal responsibilities, and they are usually appointed rather than elected.

- *Governing board* – a group of people who are ultimately accountable for providing the leadership and oversight of a legally incorporated organization. The founding members usually make up the governing board. Mintzberg (1983) identified seven roles of governing boards:

  - ✓ Selecting the CEO
  - ✓ Exercising direct control during periods of crisis
  - ✓ Reviewing management decisions and performance
  - ✓ Co-opting external influences
  - ✓ Establishing contacts for the organization and raising funds
  - ✓ Enhancing the organization's reputation
  - ✓ Giving advice to the organization

- *Policy making board* – set policy to direct and control the organization. This is essential in ensuring discipline and compliance with different laws and regulations.
- *Management board* – committee charged with overseeing the day-to-day management of the organization, particularly the organization's financial and human resources practices. It is concerned with all management issues and operational issues. This board is headed by the CEO.
- *Working board* – setting policy and day-to-day running of their organization. These are also referred to as 'hand-on boards'.

BOARD COMMITTEES

This section briefly review the four committees related to the bank failure case studies profiled in the earlier part of this book. These board committees are audit committee, remuneration committee, nomination committee, and Asset and Liability committee.

Audit Committee – made up of independent, non-executive directors with at least one individual having expertise in financial management. It is responsible for oversight of internal controls, approval of financial statements, liaison with external auditors, high level compliance matters and reporting to shareholders. In Georgia the Audit Committee must ensure that the bank's financial statements are reliable. The committee reviews the accounting policy of the bank and makes recommendations for improvement. The committee also ensures the independence, objectivity, and effectiveness of external auditors. The Audit Committee is also responsible for the review of the bank's internal control systems and risk management policy.

Remuneration Committee – decides on remuneration of executive directors, and at times other senior executives. It is responsible for formulating a written remuneration policy. It is made up of entirely independent non-executive directors. The remuneration committee is also responsible for assessing the performance of directors and senior executives.

Nomination Committee – this is involved in examining the skills, knowledge, experience and characteristics of board candidates. The Nomination committee is also involved in developing and maintaining a formal, rigorous and transparent procedure for making recommendations on appointments and reappointments to the board of the Company (the "Board"). The committee also reviews succession plans for both the executive and non-executive directors. The Nomination committee also regularly reviews the structure, size and composition (including the skills, knowledge and experience) required of the Board compared to its current position and make recommendations to the Board with regard to any changes.

Asset & Liability Committee (ALCO) - The ALCO committee provide the framework to strategically manage the bank's overall assets and liabilities for the long-term and the short term. It is also involved in establishing policies, limits and guidelines within which Asset/Liability Management (ALM) strategies are to be executed (within limits set by Board). The ALCO also conducts foreign exchange management; liquidity management; pricing (profit rate) management; and monitor the activities and review results of ALM strategy implementation and execution. It is also responsible for providing direction, guidance, and monitor performance of investment products sold to 3rd parties (client and corporate). Adequate board and management supervision is central to effective risk management and corporate governance. ALCO provides important Management Information Systems (MIS) and oversight to effectively evaluate on-and off-balance sheet risk for the bank.

BOARD STRUCTURE CASE STUDIES

Below is a review of the board structure case studies in Georgia, Canada and Germany.

CORPORATE BOARDS IN GEORGIA

Historically, Georgia is deemed a member of the Roman-German legal system. Companies are organized under a two-tier system. Fiduciary duties are fundamental to corporate governance in Georgia. Company managers in Georgia are bound to perform their duties with due diligence and care. Banks in Georgia should have an effective supervisory board that determines company strategy and vision. The Supervisory Board appoints and monitors the activities of the Management Board. The structure, composition and size of the Supervisory Board depend on the bank's size, development perspectives and risk level. The majority of the supervisory board members should be independent. "Apart from the functions determined by legislation and the bank's charter, the supervisory board's functions are developing and approving internal by-laws and regulations and instructions related to the bank's activities, succession of supervisory and management board members, remuneration and information disclosure policies" (Association of Banks Georgia, 2009). The Supervisory Board has the fiduciary responsibility of ensuring that all the bank's activities are carried out in observance of Georgian legislation.

The Management Board is the bank's executive body responsible for its day-to-day activities and accountable to the Supervisory Board and the GSM. Members of the Management Board can be elected into the Supervisory Board, if the company's charter permits. The supervisory board is also responsible for ensuring the establishment of reliable and effective internal control and risk management systems. The supervisory board should contain Audit and Risk Management committees. The audit committee is to be composed of independent members, which are defined as not being "connected to the bank and not have financial liability to the bank." There are specific qualification requirements for bank's board of directors. According to the Georgian law, the management and representation of the company shall be vested on the directors – Law of Georgia on Entrepreneurs, Article 56.1. The Regulation on Fit and Proper criteria for Administrators of Commercial Banks requires board members to have university education in economics, audit, finance, banking, business administration, accounting and law.

CORPORATE BOARD IN CANADA

Corporate governance in Canada is generally derived from the British common law model. The main focus on Canadian boards is on the oversight of management, compliance and monitoring of controls, and the provision of advice and counsel. Corporations in Canada are formed under and governed by the Canadian Business Corporation Act (CBCA) or equivalent provincial or territorial corporate legislation.

Corporate governance in Canada is also influenced by US initiatives such as Sarbanes-Oxley Act (SOX) (2002). Rules by the Canadian Securities Administrators (CSA) closely follow SOX and the consequential rules and guidelines established by the US Securities and Exchange Commission (SEC) and US Stock Exchange. Board of directors is responsible for supervising the management of the company's business and affairs. Listed public companies must have a board of directors composed of at least three independent directors in order to satisfy corporate and securities laws requirements. Some Canadian corporate statutes prescribe a minimum number of resident Canadian directors, ranging from 25% to a majority. Directors are liable to the company if they breach their fiduciary duties or the duty of care. They are also liable if they act unlawfully. Boards are required to have an audit committee. Other committees include nomination committee and remuneration committee. The Canadian Coalition on Good Governance (CCGG) considers that the directors should have a duty to be objective and independently minded. Appropriate remuneration policy should encourage these qualities. The CBCA requires that directors act honestly and in good faith with a view to the best interests of the corporation and exercise the care, diligence and skills of a reasonably prudent person in comparable circumstances. The Canadian Securities Administrators (CSA) recommends that the board of directors of a corporation adopt a written board mandate which outlines the expectations and responsibilities of directors in implementing the corporation's corporate governance approach.

Institutional shareholder groups, the media and professional director associations, such as the Institute of Corporate Directors (ICD) influences corporate governance practices in Canada. The board supervises the management of the corporation. The role of directors is one of stewardship and oversight. Under the Canadian Business Corporation Act (CBCA), directors are responsible for managing or supervising the management of the business and affairs of the corporation. The board discharges its responsibilities through majority approval of the directors at the board meetings. Responsibility for the day-to-day management of a corporation's affairs is delegated to the CEO and other senior executives who are responsible to, and report back to the board. The board may delegate certain of its responsibilities to committees of directors. However, certain responsibilities may not be delegated to a committee of the board; including (under the Canadian Business Corporation Act):

✓ Making changes to the by-laws;

- ✓ Approving the annual financial statements, a management proxy circular, a takeover bid circular or directors' circular;
- ✓ Issuing securities (except on terms already approved by the board);
- ✓ Declaring dividends; and
- ✓ Purchasing or redeeming shares of the corporation.

Boards appoint a 'Chair' from among the directors with responsibility to provide leadership to the board to enhance board effectiveness. The Board Chair is responsible for, among other things managing the board, setting the agenda, ensuring that directors are kept informed, presiding at director and shareholder meetings, and acting as a key liaison between the board and senior management.

CORPORATE BOARD IN GERMANY

German corporate governance fundamentals and practices are generally based on the provisions of the German Stock Corporation Act *(Aktiengesetz)*, the German Codetermination Act *(Mitbestimmungsgesetz)*, and the German Corporate Governance Code. Financial institutions get additional regulations from the German Banking Act *(Kreditwesengesetz)* (KWG) and EU legislation (Capital Requirements Regulation and Directive – CRR/CRD).

The German corporate governance system has three distinct characteristics: (1) concentrated ownership, (2) a dual-board structure, and (3) worker representation on the supervisory board. The German dual-board system supports a consensus approach to the corporate governance. The management board *(Vorstand)* is responsible for managing the company. The work of this board is coordinated by the Chairman of the management board. The Supervisory Board *(Aufsichtstrat)* is responsible for appointing, supervising and advising the members of the management board and is involved in strategic decision making. Supervisory Board members are elected by the company's shareholders. Enterprises employing more than 500 or 2000 employees in Germany must ensure one-third and one-half, respectively, of the supervisory board is comprises of employee representatives. The supervisory board also determines the remuneration of individual management and board members.

Germany is focusing more on board diversity, especially the promotion of women to board level. There is also an increased focus on increased professionalism of supervisory boards. The Corporate Governance Code is revised annually by a commission *Regierungskommission* which comprises managing and supervisory board representatives of listed companies and stakeholders.

CHAPTER 4

DIRECTOR PERFORMANCE AND

REMUNERATION

The profiled bank failure cases indicate the importance of measuring and monitoring the performance of directors and aligning their remuneration with the organization's strategic intent. The measurement of directors' performance and the disclosure of directors' remuneration are corporate governance topics. In most corporate governance discussions and literature there has been an exclusive focus on a particular role that board of directors perform without taking a holistic view of the board. A review of corporate governance research agendas in Chapter 1 shows that each theory of corporate governance tends to concentrate on one particular role of the board. For instance, the principal-agent theory concentrates on the monitoring role; resource-dependence theory concentrates on the provision of resources by the directors; and the stewardship theory concentrates on the board's strategic role. Director performance studies emerged as a result of the corporate scandals and failures in most economies. It also emerged from the deeper appreciation of the role of the corporation in economic transformation.

DIRECTOR PERFORMANCE

The determination of directors' performance and remuneration should not be based on recommendations from a single theory in isolation from others. This exclusionary stance perpetuates the agency problem, hence the need for the cumulative and complementary stance in the determination of directors performance and remuneration. Director performance measurement and monitoring provides a strategic opportunity in a complex business environment, hence the need to adopt a comprehensive or integrated perspective. The performance of directors should be determined based on an integrated set of board roles rather than on a single board activity. The clear definition of roles, responsibilities and expectations is an important component of determining the performance of corporate directors. The performance of directors needs to be evaluated in terms of business, organization and market dynamics. The profiled bank failure cases suggest the increased need for active directors, that is, directors who rigorously monitor the organizations they govern. Directors are classified as either executive or non-executive directors. The performance of non-executive directors takes knowledge, skills, experience and upholding to ethical values. Director performance can also be assessed in terms of providing access to resources (Pfeffer, 1972), advice and counsel (Baysinger and Butler, 1985) and developing corporate strategy.

The performance of directors can also be assessed in the context of the typology of six board roles as developed by Hung (1998). These board roles are:

- Linking the organization to the external environment
- Coordinating the interests of shareholders, stakeholders and the public
- Controlling the behaviour of management to ensure the organization achieves its objectives
- Formulation of an organization's strategy
- Maintenance of the status quo of the organization

- Supporting management in the operational activities of the business

Executive directors have the primary responsibility to direct the organization's financial health and to drive overall progress and success. These directors are part of the organization's chain command. The executive directors and the senior leaders are expected to contribute to the effectiveness of the board exploiting their skills, their expertise, and their specific knowledge in the industry where the company operates (Cadbury Report, 1992). The executive director is integral to the fulfillment of the mission of the organization. The performance of the executive directors is evaluated by the board of directors based on the predefined standards that outline the responsibilities and expectations of the executive director. The evaluation of executive directors should be continuous, forward looking and clarifying. Rather than focusing on the organization's needs and direction, the evaluation process should incorporate the external environmental factors. The director assessment process should be rigorous in order to ensure the firm establishes a strong market position. This is particularly important given the complexity of the business environment. The evaluating committee should probe the following areas:

- What the executive director achieved – Actual Results.
- How objectives were achieved – Methods and strategies used.
- Whether the director is proactive in gathering and analyzing data – Appreciative Inquiry.
- Whether the director understands the emerging trends and opportunities from technology – directors need to understand what nascent Artificial Intelligence (AI) applications might bring to their organizations.
- Whether the director modeled core values of the organization – Key values.

The free market system has strongly necessitated ignorance on the last probe due to its focus on commercialization and the executionary business approach. According to an article by Jeremy Barlow titled:

How to do an Executive Director Performance Evaluation, some key areas to assess executive director performance include:

- Administration and human resource development
- Community relations and relationship building
- Financial management
- Legal compliance
- Fundraising
- Core values
- Understanding and commitment to the organization's mission
- Assessing program development and delivery

How can the board evaluate the performance of directors?

- How you lead
- How you manage
- How you contribute

Organizations can also use the director performance measurement system according to the Performance Prism framework. The design process should be based on the five questions embodied in the Performance Prism. The directors should be actively engaged in each of the elements of the Performance Priwm.

- *Stakeholder satisfaction.* Who are the key stakeholders and what do they want and need?
- *Strategies.* Which strategies must be put in place to satisfy the wants and needs of the key stakeholders?
- *Processes.* Which processes do we need in order to effect these strategies?
- *Capabilities.* Which capabilities do we need in order to effect these processes?
- *Stakeholder contribution.* What kind of contribution do we require from our stakeholders if we are to maintain and develop these capabilities?

The director performance assessment elements can also be categorized into structure, people, process and information. However, each assessment process and questions should be customized to reflect company-specific needs and circumstances. Ongoing director performance assessment and reflection can contribute to organizational, board and individual director improvements. Organizations should adopt the methodological pluralism methodologies when conducting individual director assessments. There are different approaches to director performance assessment:

- Checklist approach
- Thought provoking evaluations
- Surveys, Group evaluations, and Personal interviews
- 360° Feedback
- External facilitators

Director performance evaluation is a key means by which boards can recognize and correct corporate governance problems, capitalize on the board as a strategic asset and add real value to organizations. The process of director performance assessment can contribute significantly to performance improvement at four levels: the board as a collective team; board/committee leadership; committees; and the individual director level. Director performance assessments provides value in terms of improved leadership, increased clarity of roles and responsibilities, improved teamwork, increased accountability, better decision making, enhanced communication, and more efficient board operations. Director performance assessment helps in identifying gaps in knowledge and expertise related to the changes in the business environment. The process helps to foster alignment and agreement on company purpose and strategy. The individual director assessment process keeps the director cognizant of the importance of his role to the overall success of the organization. The process also helps the board to identify weaknesses in leadership that have the potential to negatively affect the organization. It also helps in strengthening understanding of the business operations, customer experience and people management practices. It also enhances the relationship between the board and executives; and this relationship is a key success factor in any organization.

Though bank failures are inevitable, paying due consideration to the process of director performance measurement helps to minimize the extent of failures. The process of director assessment ensures discipline, dialogue and determination of the board of directors. This is essentially important in building trust among directors.

DIRECTOR REMUNERATION

Remuneration plays an important role in an agency relationship. Remuneration is generally a form of compensation that should rationally reflect specific risks involved in the job. The form of remuneration should be fair for both the agent and principal so that the agency relationship remains strong and effective. Executive remuneration has attracted significant interest and criticism across the globe. Fair remuneration is a prerequisite to good work performance. The main objectives of remuneration policy are to attract, retain and reward employees, managers and directors in order to motivate them to achieve the company's objectives and encourage high level performance and align the interests of contracting parties. The agency problems mainly emanate from misaligned remuneration and reward systems. Generally, remuneration is influenced by the following factors:

- The knowledge, skills and abilities required to perform the job
- The value of the job to the business
- The physical demands of the job
- The amount of training or experience required
- The working conditions associated with the job
- The amount of responsibility associated with the job
- Current market rates as a result of the supply and demand of labor.

The process of determining directors' remuneration should be rooted in the vision and organizational strategy; and should be consistent with the governance philosophy emanating from the board. The modern institution should align the policy for directors' remuneration with that for other employees. Remuneration should be clearly aligned to the performance of the organization and the value delivered to all stakeholders. The balanced approach to assessing performance and determining rewards should be part of the modern organization's remuneration philosophy. This approach runs parallel to the formulaic incentive approach. The remuneration of directors has remained firmly in the spotlight due to the increases in corporate failures. This is essential given the possessive nature among humans or agents. The four key drivers of this – namely – companies, shareholders, government and public opinion have arguably shaped the narrative in different ways. The remuneration of directors should reflect the fact that their responsibility is joint, continuous and focused on the overall health of the organization. It is therefore important to ensure that directors' remuneration is not based on short-term achievements.

In Georgia, the remuneration policy pertaining to governing board members should take into consideration the bank's corporate culture, long-term goals, strategy, and control environment. The duties and responsibilities of the members should also be taken into account when determining remuneration. It is the responsibility of the Supervisory Board to develop the remuneration policy and submit it to the general meeting of shareholders for approval.

Despite the introduction of provisions on disclosure and voting on directors' pay, transparency and interaction between companies and shareholders remains of critical importance. Continuous engagement between remuneration committees and shareholders during the remuneration strategy setting process is essential for effectiveness. Engagement and dialogue is a prerequisite to en effective director remuneration policy. There have been a number of discussions and debates on directors' remuneration in different countries for example, The Executive Remuneration Working Group (ERWG) report 2016 in UK. The ERWG issued a report in June 2016 with the recommendations for directors' remuneration:

- There should be more flexibility afforded to remuneration committees to choose a remuneration structure which is more appropriate for the company's strategy and business needs.
- Non-executive directors should serve on the remuneration committee for at least one year before taking over the chairmanship of the committee. The Financial Reporting Council should consider reflecting this best practice in the UK corporate governance code.
- Boards should ensure the company chairman and whole board are appropriately engaged in the remuneration setting process. This will ensure that the decisions of the remuneration committee are agreed by the board as whole.
- Remuneration committees need to exercise independent judgment and not be over-reliant on their remuneration consultants particularly during engagement with shareholders. To ensure that independent advice is maintained, the remuneration committee should regularly put their remuneration advice out of tender.
- Shareholder engagement should focus on the strategic rationale for remuneration structures and involve both investment and governance perspectives. Shareholders should be clear with companies on their views and level of support for the proposals.
- Companies should focus their engagement on the material issues for consultation. The consultation process should be aimed at understanding investors' views. Undertaking a process of consultation should not lead to the expectation of investor support.
- Remuneration committees should disclose the process for setting bonus targets and retrospectively disclose the performance range.
- The use of discretion should be clearly disclosed to investors with the remuneration committee articulating the impact the discretion has had on remuneration outcomes. Shareholders

will expect committees to take a balanced view on the use of discretions.

- The board should explain why the chosen maximum remuneration level as required under the remuneration policy is appropriate for the company using both external and internal (such as a ratio between the pay of the CEO and the median employee) relativities.

- Remuneration committees and consultants should guard against the potential inflationary impact of market data on their remuneration decisions.

DIRECTOR PERFORMANCE & REMUNERATION – GERMANY

The Germany corporate governance code covers a number of disclosure recommendations for German listed companies. The Code does not regulate the amount of compensation payable to senior executives. This is considered a matter for companies and their shareholders to decide. Corporate governance rules in Germany focuses on enhancing adequate disclosure so that shareholders have sufficient information available at their disposal for remuneration decision making. The German Commercial Code *(Handelsgesetzbuch)* contains the mandatory executive compensation disclosure rules. This code requires that notes to financial statements of medium-sized and large corporations must report the total remuneration of executives. Disclosable remuneration includes salaries, profit participation, options and other share-based payments, expense allowances, insurance payments, commissions and fringe benefits of every kind.

The German Commercial Code also mandates the reporting of previous members' total remuneration, including severance pay, pensions, survivors' benefits and similar payments. The full amount of accruals for pensions and expectations of pensions, together with unaccrued amounts in respect of these liabilities, should be disclosed. The Code also demands the disclosure of advances and credits to present and past directors, including the material terms and interest rates, and where applicable amounts repaid in the fiscal year and contingencies and commitments for the benefit of any such person.

The Corporate Governance Code (the Code) provides additional remuneration disclosure requirements, consisting of "recommendations" and "suggestions". Recommendations are not mandatory, but non-compliant companies must explain if they do not follow them. Failure to follow suggestions need to be disclosed. The Code does not have legal force. However, the German Statute on Transparency and Disclosure *(Transparenz und Publizitatsgesetz)* requires all German listed companies to annually declare publicly if they comply with the Code and give reasons for non-compliance. The Code's disclosure requirements reflect the dual board structure operated by German companies, comprising the Management board *(Vortstand)* and Supervisory board *(Aufsichtstrat)*. The Supervisory board determines the remuneration of individual management board members based on individual's responsibilities and performance, company performance and outlook, general economic situation, and remuneration received from other group companies.

The Code further recommends that disclosure of the compensation of management in the company's consolidated financial statements is subdivided according to fixed, performance-related and long-term incentive components. The Code further suggests that compensation of management board members should be reported on an individual basis. Management board compensation should consist of a fixed salary and variable components. Variable components should include annual and one-off components linked to company performance, and, in addition, long-term incentives such as stock options.

The compensation of the supervisory board members is determined by resolution of a general meeting of shareholders or in the company's articles of association. It is recommended that supervisory board members receive fixed and performance related compensation. The Code suggests that performance-related compensation should contain components based on the company's long-term performance. Disclosure of the compensation of supervisory board members should be given on an individual basis in the notes to the company's consolidated financial statements, subdivided according to components.

DIRECTOR PERFORMANCE & REMUNERATION – UK

The directors' remuneration disclosure requirements are contained in The Directors' Remuneration Report Regulations (2002) and The Companies Amendment Regulations. These regulations support The UK Companies Act (1985), The UK Listing Rules, and The UK Combined Code of Principles of Good Corporate Governance and Code of Best Practice (Combined Code), and The Stewardship Code.

Quoted UK companies are required to produce a "directors' remuneration report" as part of their annual reporting cycle. The remuneration report must be made by the board of directors and not by the company's remuneration committee. This is because the remuneration committee is constitutionally only a committee of the board and because the report must cover the remuneration of non-executive directors, as well as executive directors. The remuneration report is distributed to shareholders, debenture holders, and other persons entitled to receive notice of general meetings. In addition, a copy should be filed with the registrar of companies. The remuneration report must be put to an "annual advisory" shareholder vote. The remuneration report must include the following information for each person who has served as a director of the quoted company at any time during the relevant financial year: emoluments and compensation, share options, and long-term incentive schemes. The report must also include a forward-looking statement of policy on directors' remuneration for the following, and subsequent financial years.

The remuneration report must also include a performance graph. This is a line graph that shows the "total shareholder return" for the preceding five years. Total shareholder return should be calculated using a "fair method" that takes as its starting point the percentage change over the measurement period in the market price of the relevant shareholding. The directors' remuneration report is split into two parts: audit and unaudited part. The audit part contains detailed information concerning all aspects of the directors' remuneration. The unaudited part contains detailed narrative disclosures of remuneration policy and the performance graph.

DIRECTOR PERFORMANCE & REMUNERATION – CANADA

The Canadian Coalition for Good Governance (CCGG) published a policy on directors' compensation in 2011. The CCGG views directors as essential fiduciaries. According to the Policy of the Canadian Coalition of Good Governance, directors' remuneration should:

- Promote independent thinking by the directors while aligning their interests with those of the shareholders
- Reflect their expertise and time commitment to their duties
- Vary according to the duties assumed by the board
- Promote shareholding by directors
- Be the least complex possible and transparent
- Possibly be subjected to shareholder approval

In Canada, "say-on-pay" is an advisory vote whereby shareholders are provided with the right to approve, on a non-binding basis, the approach to executive management compensation. The CCGG has recommended companies to hold an annual say-on-pay advisory vote and that the board takes the results into account when considering remuneration policies, procedures and decisions. In Canada, directors' remuneration is determined by the board of directors, and shareholder approval is not required in the determination of such remuneration.

CHAPTER 5

RISK MANAGEMENT & INTERNAL CONTROLS

There has been an increase in corporate sector risk management failures in most countries during the past three decades. Despite the seemingly comprehensive risk management methodologies in the banking sector, the failures have been more pronounced in the financial services sector. There also have been many cases of non-compliance, financial fraud and resulting litigations among corporate sector players leading to increased agency problems and agency costs. These developments have thrust risk management and internal controls into the corporate governance spotlight. The management of risk is central to the corporate governance practices of banking institutions. The OECD Principles of Corporate Governance indicates that various jurisdictions have voluntarily chosen to implement effective risk management principles and practices as strategic and operational imperatives. Risk-taking is a fundamental driving force in banking operations and the cost of risk management failures is greatly underestimated.

Risk management is a core function of contemporary banking because banks as complex adaptive systems are not easily controllable. Sound corporate governance is essential in ensuring that risks are understood, managed, and communicated. The proper identification and comprehensive management of risk should be at the centre of any risk governance standards. Corporate governance standards should place sufficient emphasis on *ex ante* identification of risk. The banking market should ensure adequate strategic, compliance, innovation and operational risk management in addition to giving due consideration to both financial and non-financial risks.

The board of directors is essential in reviewing and guiding corporate policy and ensuring the implementation of appropriate risk management systems in an organization. It is the board's responsibility to set the risk policy by specifying the types and degree of risk that a company is willing to accept in pursuit of its goals (OECD Principles and Guidelines). The adoption of the Fitness Landscape Theory is essential in guiding risk management through discovery of new insights and understanding about the interrelationships between internal characteristics and external environment.

The Global Financial Crisis 2008/09 emanated from a widespread failure of risk management, primarily because risk was not managed on an enterprise basis and was not adjusted to corporate strategy. Sound corporate governance requires that the implementation of risk management adopts an enterprise-wide approach; hence the board of directors should be actively engaged in establishing and overseeing the overall risk management structure of an organization. The global financial crisis exposed a number of risk governance weaknesses in major financial institutions, relating to the roles and responsibilities of corporate boards, the firm-wide risk management function, and the independent assessment of risk.

Strategic transformational planning is essential in ensuring effective risk management and making critical decisions. This is because strategic transformational planning helps an organization to modify its business processes through adjusting policies, procedures and processes to minimize strategic, innovation, operational and other risks. Effective strategic transformational planning supports effective risk management through the determination of an organization's corporate governance structure. Strategic transformational planning supports effective risk management through its focus on the following dimensions: standardization, sophistication, structure, systemization, superiority, commitment, comprehensiveness, significance, and suppleness of the overall planning process and programmes (Miller and Cardinal, 1994). These dimensions are in line with the Enterprise-wide Risk Management approach and are essential methods of optimal solutions in banking corporate governance. The essence of strategic transformational planning and risk management is to ensure organizational effectiveness, mitigation of conflicts of interests, and proper accountability of the organization to all stakeholders.

Risk management is defined as the identification, assessment, and prioritization of risks. The ISO31000 defines risk management as the effect of uncertainty on objectives (whether positive or negative) followed by coordinated and economical application of resources to minimize, monitor and control the probability and/or impact of unfortunate events or to maximize the realization of opportunities. Common risks in banking institutions include:

- *Credit Risk* – the potential that a bank borrower or counterparty will fail to meet its obligations in accordance with the agreed terms. The bank failure case studies exhibited the increase in non-performing loans among banks due related party transactions.
- *Market Risk* – the risk of loss to an institution resulting from movements in market prices, in particular changes in interest rates, foreign exchange rates, and equity and commodity prices.
- *Operational Risk* – the risk of loss resulting from inadequate or failed internal processes, people and systems or from external events.
- *Strategic Risk* – this is the possibility of loss due to the failure by an organization to align its internal and external scenarios and events leading to a failure to achieve the organization's strategy and strategic objectives.
- *Compliance Risk* – involves the organization's exposure to legal penalties or material loss as a result of a failure to act in accordance with prescribed policies, laws and regulations.
- *Innovation Risk* – this is the risk that comes with changes in technology, products and services at both the manufacturing

and distribution stages of the value chain. The main form of innovation is the cyber risk.

- *Complexity Risk* – this is the risk resultant from the increased complexity of an organization's systems, products, technologies, processes, contracts, structures and so on. Vulnerabilities characterize organizations as they grow more complex.

Corporate governance plays an important role in enterprise risk management. The failure of financial institutions results, in part from the neglect of the basic rules, principles and practices of risk management and control. According to the OECD (2009) the common risk management problems related to corporate governance in the past financial institutions' failures includes:

- Risks were frequently not linked to strategy by aligning risks to strategy
- Risks were poorly defined in terms of context, event and consequence
- Failure by organizations to develop intelligent responses to risks
- Outsourcing important parts of the value chain without a proper governance mechanism for outsourced services

Rene Stulz (2008) pointed out five ways in which failures in financial risk management systems can be broken down:

- Failure to use appropriate risks metrics
- Mis-measurement of known risks
- Failure to take known risks into account
- Failure in communicating risks to top management
- Failure in monitoring and managing risks

The management of risks is an essential boardroom priority area and directors should pay special attention to strategic planning, succession planning, and directors' remuneration. The risk management framework should be embedded in the organization development interventions of individual banking institutions. It is essential that businesses adequately outline their risks, regularly measure the risk exposure, and persistently update their risk profile (Felton and Watson, 2002). The OECD principles state that the board should fulfill certain key functions, including reviewing and guiding corporate risk policy as well as ensuring that appropriate systems for risk management are in place and comply with the relevant laws and standards. The board has an essential responsibility to set the risk policy by specifying the types and degree of risk that a company is willing to accept in pursuit of its goals.

ENTERPRISE RISK MANAGEMENT (ERM)

This framework includes components that drive organizational effectiveness in banking and the corporate sector at large. The ERM framework as developed by COSO (Committee of Sponsoring Organizations of the Treasury Commission) has eight key components and four objectives of business. These objectives are strategic, operations, reporting and compliance. The eight components of the enterprise risk management are internal environment, objective setting, event identification, risk assessment, control activities, information and communication, monitoring, and risk response.

The Enterprise Risk Management enables the organization to pragmatically deal with uncertainty and associated risk and opportunity thus enhancing the brand value and profitability. It is an approach that enables banks to effectively deal with varied types of risks and opportunities, thus increasing stakeholder value. This approach expresses risk not just as a threat, but also as an opportunity. ERM enables banks to move away from the "silo" approach to risk management and move towards the "holistic" view of enterprise wide risks. The ERM is a key component of corporate governance as it ensures risk management is aligned to corporate strategy and objectives.

RISK MANAGEMENT AND INTERNAL CONTROLS - GEORGIA

The Supervisory Board is responsible for the establishment of effective internal controls and risk management systems. The bank's internal control and risk management systems should be evaluated at least once every year. The Supervisory Board is mandated to report the risk management and internal control, systems at the general meeting of shareholders. The Supervisory Board should contain Audit and Risk Management Committees. Committee members should get unlimited access to all internal information and bank documentation. The committee members should closely cooperate with the executive members in order to obtain information about the bank's financial position and risk level. Committee members should possess appropriate financial background and experience in the financial services sector.

Banks in Georgia should have a comprehensive risk management process that identifies, measures, monitors, and controls all major risks. The Law on Activity of Commercial Banks and the National Bank's Internal Audit Requirements for Commercial Banks require banks to set up an independent internal audit function. It is the responsibility of the Risk Management Committee to define and implement the risk management policy. The risk management policy should be approved by the Supervisory Board. The Risk Management Committee is responsible for setting risk-related limits, facilitating the establishment of risk management systems, and monitor risk management systems. The Risk Management Committee is also responsible for ensuring effective risk management as defined by the corporate governance code. There should be clear separation of responsibilities with respect to risk management between the Supervisory Board, Risk Management Committee, Audit Committee, and the External Auditors. Banks in Georgia should have an Internal Audit Department which should verify compliance with internal control measures, reveal deficiencies in the bank's operations, analyze compliance with internal policies and procedures, and review the External Auditors scope of work. The Internal Audit Department should have full, direct, and unlimited access to all structural units, bank records, bank property, and bank information systems.

CHAPTER 6

GOVERNANCE OF SERVICE PROCESSES

The extent of bank failures in most economies has indicated the complexity of governing service processes. The uniqueness of banking processes necessitated a special corporate governance consideration. A business process is a collection of linked tasks which lead to the delivery of a service or product to the customer. Business processes are essential to the survival of an organization due to their significant role in value creation. Business processes can be categorized into management processes, operational processes, and supporting processes. The proper governance of all business processes is pivotal to organizational effectiveness. Banking services fall under the service sector category particularly on the information transformation strategy. The banking sector across the globe also plays an important role in transforming people and in physical transformations. Banking falls under the service sector category due to the intangibility of the banking activities and the extensive use of automated business processes. The four main characteristics of services are prevalent in banking operations and processes. It is these service characteristics that complicate the governance of banking processes.

SERVICE CHARACTERISTICS

A service is defined as "an attempt to transform customer B's reality C, as constructed by its service provider A, at the request of B and frequently in cooperation with B." (Flikkema *et al.,* 2007). Gronroos (2007) defined a service as "a process consisting of a series of more or less intangible activities that normally, but not necessarily always, take place in interactions between the customer and service employees and/or physical resources or goods and/or systems of the service provider, which are provided as solutions to customer problems."

- *Intangibility* – unlike products, services are difficult to evaluate and the perceived risk is high. Intangibility indicates that services cannot be seen or touched as goods or products.
- *Perishability* – services cannot be inventoried, as such demand management is crucial to profitable capacity utilization.
- *Variability* – service demand varies across customers, time and from the frontline providers.
- *Simultaneous production and consumption* – customers are co-producers of the service. The participation of customers is key to success in service delivery. Services are characterized by Inseparability, that is, co-production between employee and customer/depositor.

The above-mentioned characteristics of the banking sector services makes their governance more challenging and demanding as the services need continuous monitoring and innovation. The development of a service strategy in order to champion service innovation is an essential corporate governance function. Service innovation is the driving force for sustainability in the banking industry. The governance of banking processes should hinge on a well-developed and integrative service strategy. The development of an effective service strategy is founded on methodologies such as design thinking, process mining and flowcharting. Service innovation is extremely difficult to visualize and implement, hence the necessity of process reengineering through process visualization, and process mapping and modeling. This is exacerbated by the uniqueness of banking operations and processes, and the need for service quality in the highly competitive and variable banking market. The governance of banking service processes should not exclusively focus on the service solution but should give due attention to the depositor needs and wants; hence the need to incorporate process and customer focus techniques in the development of the service strategy. The focus on the customer covers four fundamental areas that drive bank organizational effectiveness:

- *Customer information management* – this is an approach to effectively manage customer data in an enterprise. Customer information management helps in service design and delivery. The design of Customer Information Data Management System (CIDMS) helps drive superior business outcomes through better understanding of customers. Digital providers or FinTech companies helps in creating an ecosystem that fosters the collection of vast amount of customer data

- *Multi-channel integration* – involves developing more ways to connect with customers. Banking institutions are embracing the disruptive nature of financial technologies (FinTech). Embracing FinTech helps banking institutions in increasing omni-channel integration and sharpens operational excellence. This supports agility in meeting customers' ever-changing needs and wants. The different client segments of the bank calls for a multi-channel integration to service delivery in order to enhance the service encounter. The building of omni-channel retail experiences should be at the center of corporate governance discussions in banks in order to protect customer data and enhance the service encounter.

- *Operational excellence* – focuses on continuous improvement in order to meet customer expectations. Operational excellence embraces problem-solving and leadership in continuous improvement through the use of specific tools to create sustainable products or services. This demand that the organization focuses on quality, process focus, systems thinking, and value chain considerations. FinTech help in improving operational excellence and embracing FinTech should be at the heart of the banking service strategy. The use of customer care natural language processing and personal assistants is helping in enhancing operational excellence in banking.

- *Intelligent in-bound cross selling* – this encompasses selling related, supplementary products or services to customers. This is based on the multiplicity of banking service offerings and customer demands. Intelligent in-bound cross selling helps to improve revenue and customer satisfaction.

The ICT revolution makes the governance of service processes increasing complex as individual banks have to introduce technology-enabled services in order to manage risks, to compete and to survive. The governance of banking service processes should expand beyond existing services and service capability, and focus on continuously enhancing customer experience. This requires a consideration of the entire value chain in service delivery. As such technical support for services should be effective in order to ensure efficient and rapid resolution of service challenges. Service governance is essentially related to central management of the enterprise resources that span between domains or business areas. Most banking institutions have a customer experience department to operationalize the service strategy expansion. This helps in monitoring the vitality, reliability, availability, and performance of the operational systems thereby improving the service encounter on all customers. Enhancing the service encounter helps to build customer confidence in the bank and the banking system as a whole.

BANKING SERVICE STRATEGY

Banking processes are also in chaos, that is, disorganized and unordered. The governance of service processes should prioritize the development of a service strategy that is all-encompassing and support or is aligned to the overall business strategy. Collaboration between different functions is a prerequisite to the process of service strategy development in order to ensure sound implementation of the service strategy through enhanced capacity to self-organize and adapt. The service strategy will show how the bank will transform service management from an organizational capability into a strategic asset, and to think and act in a strategic manner. As a result of reliance on automated processes, banking involves a multiplicity of services, systems or processes, hence the need for the unified engineering methodology to the development and implementation of the banking service strategy. The adoption of organization development methodologies and interventions also support the effectiveness of service strategy development through diagnosis, action research and action planning. This process starts with understanding unmet and emergent customer needs, and from that vantage point emerges innovation which leads to improvements in the service strategy. This can be achieved through intense diagnosis and evaluation of the service portfolio.

A service strategy also helps to clarify the relationships between the different components of the bank and the business models, strategies or objectives they support. Banks should strive to offer consistent service in order to earn and sustain customer loyalty and trust. The corporate governance function should be strategic in the service strategy development and implementation process in order to sustain depositor confidence and organizational life.

The service strategy for banks should prioritize enhancing the bank-customer relationship. The corporate governance activities of banks should promise active customer engagement in order to make informed decisions regarding service portfolio improvements. The assurance of security of deposits and privacy should also be at the centre of the bank service strategy. This is achieved and monitored through the customer relationship management (CRM) function of the bank's service strategy. The elimination of conflict of interests between directors, managers, and other stakeholders should be at the center of the service strategy development and implementation. This is because the existence of friction and conflict between these stakeholders limits effective implementation of the service strategy. There is also an urgent need for banks to leverage on technology for efficiency and convenience in service delivery. The 2017 Retail Banking Trends and Predictions report sponsored by Kony Inc., surveyed over 500 financial institutions globally and identified the top three priorities for banks as improving the digital experience, enhancing data analytic capabilities, and finding ways to reduce costs. These elements should be integrated in the banking service strategy in order to ensure profitability and sustainability of banking processes and operations.

There is an increasing peril of disruptions in the banking sector, hence the need for banks to take more explicit strategic decisions regarding their service portfolio. The need for a truly differentiated service strategy cannot be overemphasized given the new technological developments and the increased number of banking sector entrants and global technological companies with disruptive business models. A holistic core strategic choice for existing and upcoming banking institutions involves focusing on *"manufacturing"* (creating new financial products) and on *"distribution"* (managing service delivery channels and customer relationships). The choice of the hybrid of the two is determined by the relative strength in individual *products, customer segments and internal capabilities*. It is a strategic function for corporate leaders to strengthen these three areas in banking service processes and operations because these three areas enhance sustainable competitive advantage. The **manufacturing strategy** aims to build world-class solutions for specific product needs and client segments. This demands intense and flexible product leadership and technological capabilities at organizational level. Banks can outsource external vendors to perform some of the manufacturing processes. The need for board and management commitment when outsourcing service functions is essential to effectiveness and to minimize the agency-problem. Banking service outsourcing is a key corporate governance function as it requires extensive strategic assessment, financial evaluation and a true commitment to cooperative relationships with vendors. However, outsourcing creates opportunities for managers to further their self-interests through self-dealing transactions at the expense of the bank. The outsourcing-induced self-dealing transactions that lead to agency problems include the 'padding' of budget requests during the assessment and evaluation stage and eventual transitioning to outsourced services. These transactions negatively affect the bank's liquidity and viability as they increase agency costs.

The **distribution model** offers a full product suite, tailored to particular industry or customer profiles with a combination of non-bank, white-label solutions and partnerships with other financial services providers. This model demands customer analytics, strong customer relationships, simple channels, and economies of scope. The distribution model is at the centre of the service encounter due to the interaction between the customer and the service or products from the manufacturing model. In view of the mutually exclusive relationship between the manufacturing and distribution models, the board should play an oversight role in both manufacturing and distribution strategies. This is achieved through the synergizing and linkage building roles of the board and senior leaders in an organization.

Sustainability is a key measure of bank effectiveness. To achieve the bank sustainability objective, sound governance of banking service processes is a necessity. The governance process should involve the following:

- *Stakeholder engagement* – the bank should engage all its stakeholders in order to make effective service strategy decisions. It is the responsibility of the management board to ensure effective stakeholder engagement.
- Clear definition of all the bank services, that is, the service portfolio. The service portfolio should cover the three main categories of services

  ✓ *Service pipeline* – these are proposed services or the services under development. This category determines the strategic direction of the enterprise and should be aligned with the process and service visualization techniques that should be embedded in the manufacturing model.

  ✓ *Service catalogue* – this include the bank's live or available services for deployment. The service catalogue determines service encounter and the Key Performance Indicators (KPIs), hence its connection to the distribution model.

These services are integrated in the digital performance dashboard for continuous monitoring and operational excellence.

✓ *Retired services* – these are decommissioned services. The reasons for decommissioning certain services should inform and guide the development and implementation of the distribution and manufacturing strategies in order to ensure service excellence.

- Critical analysis of the service portfolio in order to find the perspectives, plans, patterns and positions. This act of critical analysis of the bank's value proposition helps the board and senior management in making informed strategic decisions regarding the banking service processes and initiatives. There are three strategic categories of service investments:

  ✓ *Run The Business (RTB)* – this is centered on maintaining the status quo on service operations. This is benchmarked on operational efficiency through key business processes and enabling technologies. This focuses primarily on the service catalogue and the bank's position of being 'suppliers' rather than 'orchestrators' of banking services. The manufacturing model under the RTB lacks service innovation capabilities; hence organizations that dwell on this category of service investment will not survive for long in the current dynamic and competitive business environment.

  ✓ *Grow The Business (GTB)* – intended to grow the organization's scope of services. This calls for better understanding of the customers, competitors, markets and new product development. It also encompasses risk resilience, and constantly updating the service pipeline category of the service portfolio. The Evolution business model drives the Grow The Business (GTB) service investments.

  ✓ *Transform The Business (TTB)* – encompasses moving into new market spaces, for example, through the blue ocean strategy. This requires investments in service transformation planning, through the hybrid of manufacturing and distribution strategies. It involves being orchestrators of the banking services. The Disruption business model primarily drives the Transform The Business (TTB) service investment.

✓ Approval of service portfolio by the board of directors, specifically the governing board. Empirical studies suggest that there are six outcomes from the service authorization process: Renew, Replace, Retain, Refactor, Retire, Rationalize.

- The board should be actively involved in the formulation of the service strategy based on the innovation process and customer needs assessments. This process will involve exploration, creation, and reflection on the service package. The whole process demands decision engineering techniques in order to make informed decisions. A service package is a bundle of goods and services provided by an organization. The features of the service package influences consumer behavior about service delivery, hence it is a key factor in enhancing the service encounter. The bank service package should be well-thought out and streamlined in order to create competitive advantage. The service package includes:

✓ *Supporting Facility* – the structure or physical resources to support service delivery. The supporting facility is closely connected to the manufacturing model.

✓ *Facilitating Goods* – the goods that are used to ensure service delivery. It encompasses the material that is consumed by the customer or items provided by the consumers. Facilitating goods supports the manufacturing and distribution model of the bank.

✓ *Information* – data provided by the customer to enable efficient and customized service delivery. The information element is essential for operational excellence at both the manufacturing and distribution stages of service delivery. Information and data is the life blood of success in banking.

✓ *Explicit Service* – these are the benefits that the customer quickly notices by the senses and are based on the intrinsic or essential features of the service.

✓ *Implicit Services* – these are psychological benefits or extrinsic features which the consumer may sense only vaguely.

- Implementation and monitoring are essential in the process of service strategy design. The adoption of process measurement and project management methodologies is crucial to the effectiveness of the implementation of the service strategy.

SERVICE INNOVATION

Service innovation is a key factor in creating sustainable competitive advantage and is a propellant for business growth, development and transformation. It is through service innovation that an organization can sustain its manufacturing and distribution model. The recognition of the significance of service innovation in banking helps improve corporate performance and the creation of core competencies for achieving and sustaining competitive advantage. The banking sector is characterized by unprecedented growth, new regulations, new systems and new policies. Service innovation is essential to the success of any bank as it enhances depositor satisfaction and confidence, and drives competitiveness. The board and executives should be actively involved in the identification and definition of service innovation dimensions in the bank. The capabilities for managing service innovation are therefore a corporate governance strategic consideration. The need for service innovation in the banking sector is necessitated by the intensity of global competition, impact of structural change, and the adoption of new technologies. It is essential for banks to embrace and partner with FinTech companies in order to ensure service innovation through expansion of products and services, increasing customer base, agility in responding to competition, decrease IT infrastructure costs, and leverage existing data and analytics. Prioritizing the innovation process is key for individual bank's sustainability. Empirical literature indicates that there are three main approaches that should guide the governance of the banking service processes innovation:

- *Assimilation Perspective* – "service innovation is not distinctive; it can be studied and organized in ways familiar from analysis of manufacturing." The focus is mainly on technology innovation.
- *Demarcation Perspective* – "services are qualitatively distinctive especially due to features of intangibility, interactivity, etc; hence the need for different forms of innovation and innovation processes."
- *Synthesis Perspective* – it involves bringing together neglected aspects of innovation process.
- There are six dimensions to exploring service innovation. These are referred to as the Six-Dimensional Service Innovation model elements of Hertog (2010):
- *Service concept* – this is also referred to as the service offering (Frei, 2008). It describes the value that is created by the service provider in collaboration with the customers. This can be evidenced by the service portfolio and service package.
- *Customer interaction* – this covers the role of the customer in value creation. It covers communication, co-design, customization or co-production (Normann, 2002)
- *Value chain/System* – this involves the new business partners involved in service innovation. This can be strengthened by improved stakeholder engagement.
- *Revenue Model* – encompasses models to distribute costs and revenues. Managers must be creative enough to develop appropriate revenue models of service innovation. Examples include e-technological development and improvements in distribution channels.
- *Delivery (Organization)* – covers the human element to service delivery including organization structure and culture. It also

involves optimizing on capabilities of individuals and teams through training and education.

- **Delivery (Technology)** – this dimension covers the systems and processes in service delivery such as Automated Teller Machines (ATMs). The systems help in ensuring data is captured accurately.

In view of the close connection of business functions and processes, the banking service management model should be fact-based, integrated and well-structured. The integrated system should support service innovation through focusing on the service concept, the customer interface, the service delivery system/organization, and technological options (Hertog, 2010). The eight main components of an Integrated Service Management (ISM) approach are:

- *Product Elements* – involves selecting the core products and defining supplementary service elements. This falls under the manufacturing strategy of service design.
- *Place, Cyberspace, and Time* – focuses on ensuring speed and convenience to customers. This component deals with the definition of the channels of delivery. This falls under the distribution model of service design.
- *Promotion and Education* – enhances communication through the different channels, hence falls under the distribution model.
- *Price and other user outlays* – organizations should properly manage expenditures and other outlays incurred by customers. The focus should therefore be enhancing the manufacturing and distribution models of service delivery.
- *Process* – involves definition of the methods and sequence of actions in service delivery. This is an essential component of both the manufacturing and distribution strategies.
- *Productivity and Quality* – this is an essential component of the manufacturing model, and involves the transformation of inputs into outputs.
- *People* – organizations should ensure direct interaction between customers and employees. The HR Management

Systems should be enhanced to ensure effective manufacturing and distribution of the services.

- *Physical Evidence* – involves enhancing the appearance of the supporting facility and facilitating goods and creating meaningful symbols.

Banking corporate governance should focus on redesigning the operating model in response to the ever-changing operating environment. This involves the avoidance of reliance on generic industry benchmarks and focus on the emerging trends and market disruptions. There is need to constantly rethink the role, structure and processes of critical banking functions such as IT, Treasury, Lending, Risk, Retailing, and Compliance. Corporate governance should focus on designing and building an adaptive operating model that will sustain business growth and transformation, rather than the Run The Business (RTB) service investment approach. The governance of service processes is extremely complex, hence the need for directors to establish measurements, policies, standards, and control mechanisms that drives organizational effectiveness. Boards should ensure that their banks integrate to innovate, create an IT culture that supports service innovation, and constantly evaluates emerging technologies. These instruments are essential in order to ensure sound corporate governance premised on Grow The Business (GTB) and Transform The Business (TTB) service investments. There is need to identify various control points across the different functions of the bank. "A control point is a decision checkpoint that provides an opportunity to measure adherence to the established processes, whether you are on track to meet the targets and goals you have established and then decide whether the way the processes are executed or managed needs adjusting." A control point is a critical element of process measurement and project management methodologies. Corporate governance should therefore integrate the Evolution and Disruption Models in order to ensure organizational effectiveness.

There are four building blocks that support any governance model and as such should be adopted in contemporary banking in order to mitigate or minimize bank distress and/or bankruptcy:

- *Compliance* – this process provides the mechanisms for review and approval or rejection within criteria established in the governance framework of the manufacturing and distribution strategies. This is supported by the board's role as stewards of the enterprise and as guardians of strong governance.
- *Vitality* – the vitality process maintains the applicability of the governance model by requiring it to be current and reflect business as well as ICT directions and strategies. The strategist and futurist roles of the board are essential in ensuring vitality within an organization.
- *Exceptions and Appeals* – allows a project to request and gain an exception for the use of a solution, process, policy, investment or design that is not compliant with the established governance framework. This aligns to the Risk and Scenario Planner role of the board of directors.
- *Communications* – aimed at educating and communicating the governance model across the organization and all stakeholders. The board of directors is the public face, global advocate and model of values and core values.

The governance of service processes requires more than just focusing on organizational components. It also requires support: skill support, organizational change management support, and infrastructure and tools support. Required skills in the banking sector include business, finance, banking, accounting, human resource management, organization development, and IT. The essential change management elements include governance planning, talent management, service ownership, business responsiveness, and organizational design. These skills should be cultivated in the board and executive committee structures.

Bain & Company identified five areas of the operating model that connects strategy and execution. This is in view of the significance of the organizational alignment in organizational effectiveness.

- Structure – the matrix of products, geographies and segments that will work best for manufacturing and distribution of banking services.
- Accountabilities – aligning roles and responsibilities to excel in key capabilities.
- Governance – speeding up the critical decisions in capital allocation, IT, Capex, product design, and vendor choice.
- Ways of working – calibrating a culture that fosters collaboration across functions and with vendors
- Capabilities – combining people, processes and technology to reinforce the elements of strategy.

The above mentioned five areas are essential to the evolution of banking processes and such should be embedded in banks' organization development practices. The Bain & Company also identified five critical areas for bank sustainability:

- Customer focus
- Outside expert partners
- Agility
- Technology design
- Workforce evolution

According to the Bain & Company, the key corporate governance questions for redesigning the operating model to suit evolving strategy are:

- How should we adapt our organizational structure? Should we design fit-for-purpose operating models for different business areas?
- Do we know what capability gaps exist and how to close them?
- Does our IT respond to clearly defined business unit requirements?
- What workforce changes need to occur and how will we attract and retain the talent needed?
- How do we finance the change? Is our corporate centre set up to actively prioritize resources?

GOVERNANCE OF OUTSOURCES SERVICES

There are two main forms of governing outsourced services: Traditional Theory and Hybrid Governance Theory. The traditional theory is hierarchical and considers an arm's length relationship between the customer and the vendor. The hybrid governance theory seeks to realize the control, goal alignment, and improved coordination associated with retaining an activity internally while benefitting from potentially superior skills and cost position of specialized, external organizations. It focuses on long-term, collaborative partnerships. The evolution of banking processes calls for the adoption of the Hybrid Governance Theory. The theory is mode democratic as it promotes collaboration and participation of all the contracting parties in decision making, thereby minimizing or eliminating agency costs.

In view of the mega-disruptions as a result of the use of machines in banking, the governance framework needs to also adopt computational ethics. Computational ethics seeks to provide machines not with "right" or "wrong" choices but with acceptable behavioral parameters within society (Lauterbach and Bonime-Blanc, 2016). The governance mechanism should also take into consideration the social, economic and environmental implications of technology in banking.

The next section discusses banking service strategy at micro and macro levels in different countries. The consideration of environmental issues by France has necessitated the inclusion of the French banking service strategy case study below.

BANKING SERVICE STRATEGY – GERMANY

The service structure and financial service infrastructure in Germany is non-discriminatory and advanced. Though reportedly "over-banked", Germany has a modern banking sector which distribute financial products and services via multi-channels such as Automated Teller Machines (ATMs), Mobile-banking, and online banking.

Germany has a "three pillar" banking system which is made up of private commercial banks, co-operative banks, and the public banks. The three types of banks offer a full range of services to their customers. The banking services offered include special credit services such as financing of homeowner mortgages, guarantees to small businesses, and funding projects in disadvantaged regions. The service strategy in Germany is influenced by increasingly fierce competition and the increasing demands from customers due to digitization.

The Germany banking customers are increasingly expecting seamlessly integrated solutions which are easy to use. The banking strategy is also influenced by modularization as banks are no longer the undisputed owner of the customer interface, product supplier and provider of the underlying platforms in one. The banking industry is increasingly developing into an ecosystem in which banks may only play one of the various banking roles. The service strategy for individual banks in Germany encompasses determining sustainable business models for both evolution and disruption. The banking service strategy integrates elements of acting as *suppliers* or as *orchestrators*. "Suppliers provide financial products and services, and act as a link between market actors and leverage specialist knowledge or economies of scale. Orchestrators control the interface to the customer and can even bundle complex solutions from different suppliers into a seamless customer experience."

Empirical studies states that the evolution scenario encompasses local banks aspiring to leverage their local presence and become a *"local incumbent"*, who covers all the financial needs within an economically strong metropolitan region, or slim down to an *"ascetic banking model"* for regions with lower economic activity. Banks which are active in multiple regions will either need to become "client champions" or focus on a *"monoliner model"*.

The disruption model takes a radical approach to service strategy as banks aspire to become a "guide in the digital jungle" for their clients, a *"risk partner"*, who is able to absorb and process highly structured risks, or an *"invisible bank"* which is deeply integrated into "plumbing" of other services so that clients do not even recognize the involvement of a bank anymore. There is considerable risk for banks to turn into *"museum banks"* that continue to try in vain to cover all products and the entire value chain themselves.

The banking service strategy in Germany is therefore based on two key levers: cultural flexibility and the creation of innovation-friendly environment. The innovation mindset is essential to corporate governance as directors shift from traditional "cost reduction" and "growth strategy" programmes to become more nimble and audacious in managing change. There is a significant increase in market infrastructure providers and international technology companies in Germany. Germany has significant capital market infrastructure providers (exchanges, clearing houses, securities services providers, and custodians); information service providers, data analytics providers and research boutiques. These institutions have increased their financial services market share at the expense of banks. Germany banks benefit from efficient use and commercialization of large amounts of data and the central positioning within an ecosystem. The banks also capitalize on the number of market infrastructure providers. Germany banks face competition from global technology companies such as Alibaba, Amazon, Facebook, PayPal and Google. These companies are revolutionizing direct access to banking products through their globally established customer platforms. These groups offer efficient matching and settlement processes and their technological capabilities and financial resources make them a significant threat to Germany banks' hence their influence on banking service strategy.

BANKING SERVICE STRATEGY - FRANCE

Empirical literature states that the French banking system underwent a fundamental structural reform in 1984, which removed the distinction between commercial banks and merchant banks and grouped most financial institutions under a single supervisory system. Banks in France adopt a balanced universal banking model that offers a full range of banking, financial, and insurance solutions to meet the specific needs of individuals, businesses, professionals, and non-profit organizations. The service strategy for most banks is informed by online banking, digital innovation and continuous development of multi-channel platforms for customers with high performance mobile apps and a strong social media presence. There is also an increasing focus on the development strategy of international banking networks. The financial sector has also committed to take action on climate change, with the aim of making financial flows consistent with the Paris Agreement's climate change goals.

BANKING SERVICE STRATEGY – ZIMBABWE

The Zimbabwean banking system is modeled on the British system. The banking system is composed of commercial banks, merchant banks, building society, the People's Own Savings Bank, development financial institutions, and microfinance institutions. The financial inclusion strategy aims to ensure the existence of an inclusive financial sector by all citizens. The service strategy for most banks in Zimbabwe is driven by deposit mobilization, strategic partnerships, investment in digital platforms, and e-channels, and transactions.

CHAPTER 7

THE MIDDLE MANAGEMENT REVOLUTION IN CORPORATE GOVERNANCE

Corporate governance is mainly associated with the board of directors and senior managers or executive leaders. This is mainly informed by the role of these groups in strategic thinking and strategic leadership. However, the middle management plays an important role in the success of the corporate governance activities of an organization. The principal-agency problem is founded on the separation and divergence of interests between managers (agents) and shareholder (principal). Most corporate governance literature focuses on the principal and neglects the agent's role in corporate governance. The middle management is at the center of a hierarchical organization, subordinate to the senior management but above the lowest levels of operational staff. The concept of management has become universal and no organization can survive without it. Management consists of getting things done through others by directing their efforts in an integrated and coordinated manner towards achieving business objectives. The Figure below indicates that an organization is made up of lower level employees, middle managers, senior managers and executives. The executives could include the CEO, Chief Finance Officer (CFO), Chief Operating Officer (COO), Chief Talent Officer (CTO) and other C-suite leaders.

The C-suite leaders rely mainly on Executive Information systems, whilst the senior and middle managers makes use of Management Information Systems in decision making. The lower level employees are mainly involves in transaction processing or the operational activities of the firm. The middle managers play a significant role in ensuring effective online analytical processing, decision engineering, process mapping and modelling, and benchmarking with the help of the MIS. The information from MIS is useful for the executives to make informed decisions.

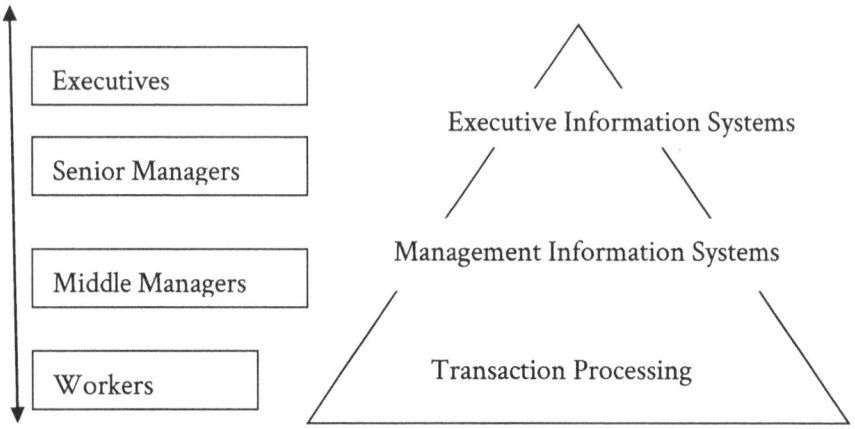

The revolution of the middle management function is a corporate governance necessity given the significant functions of middle-level managers. Though the board dominates corporate governance discussions, management is in the chain of command and is the source of the agency problem. Generally, the management process encompasses planning, organizing, coordinating, controlling and directing. A failure to incorporate the middle management revolution in corporate governance creates severe agency problems and increases agency costs due to the perpetuation of interest divergence between the principal and the agent. The main functions of middle managers are:

- Interpreting policies – this involves understanding and interpreting organizational strategy

- Preparing organizational set-up – this encompasses acting as a change agent and engaging in the actual activities of the business in order to grow and transform the business. Managers are also involved in proposing development strategies to the directors and senior leaders.
- Appointing employees and facilitating knowledge sharing
- Guiding employees and developing core competencies
- Motivating employees and maximizing performance potential
- Creating cooperation among different divisions

Mary C. Niles identified the following six functions of middle management:

- To execute the various functions of the organization so that the top management gets enough time to look after their responsibilities
- To cooperate among themselves, with top management and the supervisors so that the organization functions smoothly
- To understand the interlocking of departments in major policies and procedures
- To achieve coordination between the different parts of the organization
- To develop and train employees in the organization for better functioning and for filling up vacancies in future
- To build company spirit where all are working to provide a product or service wanted by the public.

In line with the systems thinking model of Organization Development, this chapter is founded on the unified governance function. The unified governance function is divided into two organizational functions: *governance*, making decisions for protecting owners' interests; and *management*, coordinating business activities and managing relationships in a most efficient way with the purpose to attain objectives and goals set by governance. Corporate board of directors relies on the middle management function for accurate, timely information on the company's strategic initiatives, risk, controls, and challenges. These are submitted through a management proxy circular to board to facilitate the development and eventual implementation of a strong business case or service strategy. In turn, middle managers rely on directors for wisdom and judgment. The board is responsible for the approval of the management circular.

The development of management proposal for the various organizational projects is an essential function of management. These proposals should be developed in response to the outcomes of the board's strategy development and strategic decision making. In view of the agency problem, the management proposals should be examined and approved by the board. The development of management proposals and determination of strategic alternatives is a key function of management and as such require participatory approaches in order to ensure effectiveness. The board in most cases plays a "rubber-stamping" role as per the Management-Hegemony theory. The revolution of the middle management function is a corporate governance necessity since managers effectively control the organization. The Management-Hegemony Theory states that organizational control in the modern organization is ceded to a group of professional managers. The revolution of the middle management function will enable organizations to inevitably resist the increased involvement of the board in all strategic decisions by promoting collaboration with managers. The professional managers in the modern organization are responsible for strategic decisions and the board is used as a managerial tool to support the professional managers and for performance evaluation. The board is responsible for strategic leadership and oversight of the organization. The board therefore engages in a supporting role to the group of professional managers.

The middle management revolution should be at the centre of corporate governance literature and discussions because management has a role in the appointment of directors and the fact that directors are co-opted in the organization. The board of directors is also constrained from making independent decisions because they have to rely on information supplied by management. Without the management function, the board of directors lack required knowledge to make effective decisions. The significant role of management can be determined from the roles of the governing boards as *ratifiers* of decisions (Jensen, 1983), *controllers* in monitoring and implementation of decisions (Fama and Jensen, 1983), and *supporters* of management (Aram and Covey, 1986).

Middle managers have an information privilege and hold special positions in an organization with regards to processes and customers. A failure to incorporate middle managers in the corporate governance agenda of an organization will lead to the ideas of the Entrenchment Theory. The theory describes the deviant strategies of management and their influence on organizational effectiveness. Managers will tend to enhance their compensation, their prestige and their control of the organization's resources at the expense of the organization and other stakeholders. The managers can also reduce the risky investments in order to maximize their results at the expense of the organization. This is mainly evident in banking operations and when outsourcing services; hence the need for a Hybrid Governance model.

The banking service is characterized by simultaneous production and consumption. Management plays an important role in enhancing the service encounter through the active engagement with customers and vendors as supported by the advocacy capabilities of managers. This is in line with the principle of *Management-By-Walking Around* (MBWA). The process of enhancing the service strategy, developing the service portfolio and ensuring service innovation depends on the management rather than the governance function. The linking and support role of directors is essential in reinforcing and generating commitment from managers and other key stakeholders. The management function is essential in implementing the service strategy and designing the service package. Effective governance of service processes requires the management function to establish measurements; develop policies, standards and control mechanisms for the entire organization. The monitoring of control points is also a responsibility of management because of their technical capabilities.

The governing board should play a role in avoiding management entrenchment and managerial opportunism as a result of moral hazard with information asymmetries. This is achieved through enhancing the organizational capabilities.

In view of the rising feature of managerialism, were power over the enterprise is concentrated in the hands of senior managers, who enjoy large discretion in decision making, the task of corporate governance mechanisms is to control managerial discretion to assure that the 'right' decisions are made, or at least that the managers are kept within measurable bounds. Corporations in America are run under the supervision of a single board. German corporations are organized under the Stock Corporation Act and have a two-tier system. In Zimbabwe, corporations follow the two-tier board system. The middle management should be actively involved at all the three strategic categories of service investments: Run The Business (RTB), Grow The Business (GTB), and Transform The Business (TTB). However, most governance literature places management function exclusively on the Run The Business (RTB) category. Besides being actively involved in enhancing the operational efficiency of the organization, the corporate governance mechanisms should also incorporate the middle management function in growing and transforming the business.

CHAPTER 8

BANK PERFORMANCE MEASUREMENT AND MANAGEMENT

"The biggest problem in banking is measuring performance. Professional tennis players operate on a level playing field with their opponents, using the same surface and balls, the same wind speed. Their performance can be measured. But now you are the CEO at a major British Bank. Tomorrow the pound crashes and your bank have the worst year in history. That is far beyond your control" (Wawoe, 2013).

The profiled bank failures advertised the inadequacy of performance measurement and management methods in banks. There is need for discovery and prediction techniques in performance measurement, rather than the exclusive reliance on historical reports. The governance of banking institutions is too complex as a result of innumerable unknowns and factors beyond an individual bank CEO's control. The issue of determining effective metrics for bank performance and managing the performance of the bank is central to corporate governance. The adoption of effective measures of bank performance is central to individual bank profitability and sustainability. The Global Financial Crisis 2008/09 also revealed significant weaknesses in the performance metrics and performance management techniques being used by the financial community in all countries. The integration of corporate management and corporate governance is essential in determining the performance targets, assessing bank performance, analyzing performance, analyzing variances, and predicting performance thereby implementing effective and informed controls. Corporate governance should ensure the alignment of the performance management system with all the organization's structures and activities. Performance measurement is a prerequisite for increasing firm performance. It is essential that banks and/or any other institution devise performance management criteria that is clear, smart, easy to understand and implement, and healthy (Parker, 2000).

The main or traditional measures of bank performance are profitability and productivity. Other determinants of bank performance include the share price and the present bank valuation. The importance of banking sector soundness and profitability in terms of economic growth calls for continued monitoring of individual bank's performance. The management of bank performance should refrain from relying on the executionary approach and the exclusive focus on the traditional and economic measures of performance.

Sound corporate governance is a necessity for bank soundness and profitability because it reduces the frequency and volumes of related party transactions and 'self-dealing' practices, hence a reduction in agency costs. Self-dealing practices and related party transactions are the nemesis of bank effectiveness because they are sub-optimal from efficiency perspective. Banks should focus on reducing such transactions and practices. The soundness of banks and their governance can be determined as the capacity to generate sustainable revenues and profits. Bank profitability is essential to strengthening the bank's balance sheet and enhancing sustainability for the bank through the proper investment of retained earnings. Literature indicates that the main drivers of bank performance are risk taking, leverage, revenue growth, and efficiency. The revenue growth drivers consider the volatility and composition of the bank's earnings. Banks efficiency is a measure of the bank's ability to continually generate revenue from its assets. Efficiency measure takes into consideration both the top-line and the bottom-line of the bank's financial statements. Efficiency is the fundamental element of performance. Risk taking is reflected in the necessary adjustments to earnings for the undertaken risks to generate them. Leverage acts as a multiplier as it significantly improves the bank's operating results. These measures focus on the economic results of the bank. A more holistic approach to performance measurement and management is required in the banking industry.

CATEGORIES OF BANK PERFORMANCE MEASURES

There are three categories of bank performance measures: traditional, economic and market-based measures. The **traditional or conventional measures** of corporate performance include Return on Assets (RoA), Return on Equity (RoE) and the Net Interest Margin (NIM). The RoA is the net annual revenue divided by total assets. It indicates the level of bank profitability and the bank management's ability to generate revenue through the utilization of available assets. It therefore is an indicator of management's efficiency in generating net revenue from the available resources.

RoA = Net Annual Income/Average Total Assets

Return on Equity (RoE) is a measure of the total profit earned by the company in relation to total shareholders' equity. It determines what the shareholders anticipate in return for their investment.

RoE = Net Income afterTax/Total Equity Capital

RoE shows how efficiently managers are using shareholders funds.

The Net Interest Margin (NIM) refers to a proxy for the revenue generation capacity of the bank based on its financial intermediation function. It is a ratio that determines the difference between the bank's interest income from loans and securities, and interest cost of its borrowings. The NIM reflects the bank's efficiency and overall cost of the intermediation services. This ratio is directly related to profitability.

NIM = Net Interest Income/Assets (or interest-bearing assets)

Economic and accounting measures of bank performance are founded on the shareholder wealth maximization objective. The economic measures seek to assess the economic results of the firm relative to its economic assets during a predefined period, mainly the fiscal year. Empirical literature indicates that the economic indicators are divided into two:

- indicators related to the total return of an investment, based on the concept of an "opportunity cost", for example Economic Value Added (EVA)
- indicators related to the underlying level of risk associated with bank's activity. This encompasses an analysis of the "complex trade-off between growth, return and risk; favoring the adoption of risk-adjusted metrics."

Market-based measures characterize the way capital markets value a company's activities relative to the estimated accounting value. Examples of these measures include Total share return, Price Earnings ratio, Price to book value ratio, and credit default swap.

Contemporary businesses are expected to focus on not only the economic measures or responsibilities but to incorporate legal, ethical and philanthropic responsibilities that cover societal norms, or standards. Banks must recognize and respond to environmental changes as determined by industry trends, market structure, competition, and public expectations in terms of terms of the societal and ethical performance. Carroll (1970) emphasized the increasing importance of examining corporations not just on their accounting or market-based success, but also on non-economic criteria. This is in line with the Triple Bottom Line reporting requirement in which firms should report on people, planet and profit.

The bank failure cases profiled in the first part of this book indicate that banks adopted the conventional measures of performance. These measures heavily rely on accounting indicators, while ignoring the non-financial indicators. There was also a focus on the internal analysis rather than incorporating the external factors. It is stated that merely analyzing economic and accounting indicators does not constitute an effective strategy for financial institutions, since their performance interlinks financial indicators with non-financial indicators (Sagar and Rajesh, 2008). As a result, financial performance is determined by too many intangible business processes and performance indicators. Zhang and Longyi (2009) regard the traditional measures of performance as inadequate and point out the following deficiencies in traditional performance measures: (i) too heavy a focus on financial indicators, while ignoring the intangible indicators; (ii) too much focus on the internal analysis of operating conditions, while excluding external factors; and (iii) too great an emphasis on traditional assets, while neglecting intangible assets. The main limitation of traditional performance measures is the use of raw accounting data (Martin, Salas and Saurina, 2007).

The conventional performance measures also emphasize traditional assets while neglecting intangible assets (Zhang and Longyi, 2009). An effective organization "realizes that intangible assets like brand value, community trust, license to operate, access to capital, and consumer passion require more than a narrow focus on shareholder value creation. Also needed is stakeholder value creation" (Cooperrider, 2012). Though banks' fixed assets are important, the banking sector is a knowledge intensive industry, and financial knowledge, intellectual resources and other intangible assets are also relevant performance drivers. Banks' complexity has increased considerably, and intangible assets have become an important driver of performance. The value of a bank is made up of material assets, intangible assets and rents from market power (Martin and Salas, 2007). The adoption of the Balanced Scorecard (BSC) as developed by Kaplan & Norton (1992) helps to bridge the gap of conventional performance measures. Sagar and Rajesh (2008) additionally suggest that certain commonly used financial ratios provide indications of the contribution of intangible assets. For example, the growth rate of deposits is a good indicator of customer confidence in the financial institution. Another indicator is the growth rate in loans, which illustrates the customer preference for the services of a specific bank.

Bank performance measurement can also be done through market discipline and disclosure. Market discipline is regarded as the ultimate performance indicator in a market economy. Meaningful disclosure is a prerequisite for effective market discipline as it allows all stakeholders to conduct personal assessments of bank's risk profile and performance. Transparency is essential in bank performance measurement. It would also be beneficial to enhance transparency of financial reporting, which does not mean increasing the amount of reported or publicly available information. As a matter of fact, it is quite easy to get lost in the complexity of reporting and disclosures and fail to effectively address their objectives.

The measures of bank performance can be divided into internal and external metrics. **Internal determinants** of bank effectiveness focus on specific features such as bank size, capital management efficiency, risk management capacity, loan and deposits. **The external determinants** are derived from the bank's economic and regulatory environment. The performance of banks is also greatly influenced by management policies, decisions, objectives and actions. These are reflected in the bank's operating results. "Management decisions, particularly regarding loan portfolio concentration are an important factor contributing to bank performance" (Zimmerman, 1999). The performance of banks can also be assessed through interest spread and overall liquidity. According to Jaffee (1989), the following factors affect the interest spread within banks:

- the degree of market concentration;
- regulatory constraints that prohibit the bank from undertaking certain profitable activities and increase the cost of providing acceptable activities;
- higher credit risk, and
- exposures to interest rate risk.

Another key determinant for improving bank performance is the ability to manage operating expenses. Operating expenses falls under the controllable costs category and as such if operating expenses are well managed, bank performance will be enhanced. The main operating cost for banks is the interest expenses. A rise in interest expenses leads to lower rate return on equity capital. Goddard et al., (2004) indicated the use of capital structure in determining bank performance. The most ideal source of funding banks is deposits. Banks should strive to maintain an optimal capital structure in order to improve and sustain performance. The CAMEL framework is also used to proxy bank specific determinants of effectiveness. CAMEL is the acronym for "Capital Adequacy, Asset Quality, Management Efficiency, Earnings Ability, and Liquidity."

CHAPTER 9

ORGANIZATION DEVELOPMENT (OD)

The study of successful organizational change and performance has assumed a heightened attention over the past three decades. Organizational change is inevitable considering that the business operating environment has become highly volatile, unpredictable, and uncertain. "It has become increasingly apparent that strategies for organizational change have become an aphorism for maintaining success and creating competitive advantage in complex organizations" (Wilson, 1992). Organizations' dynamism as a result of the rapid changes in the internal and external business environment make organization development a strategic corporate governance element. As a result of the rapidly expanding scale and scope of change and its accelerating pace, organization life is increasingly becoming impermanent and transient; hence according to complexity science organizations are complex adaptable systems. The view of an organization as a network of multiple, and fairly autonomous agents calls for a corporate governance framework that is informed by OD principles, practices and interventions.

As highlighted in the previous Chapters, corporate governance is primarily concerned with how an organization is managed and directed. Organization Development (OD) is a field of research, theory, and practice dedicated to expanding the knowledge and effectiveness of people; and the improvement of processes, systems, and structures to accomplish more successful organizational change and performance. It is a process of continuous diagnosis, action planning, implementation and evaluation, with the goal of transferring knowledge and skills to organizations, improve their capacity for solving organizational problems and managing change. It is through the adoption of the organization development science, theory and practices that organizations can sustain the evolution and disruption models to organizational effectiveness.

Chapter 11 discusses the methods of optimal solutions and most of these methods support the OD interventions. The bank failures and other corporate collapses experienced in most economies could be minimized or avoided through the application of organization development theory into the fabric of corporate governance. This is primarily because organization development focuses on aligning organizations with their rapidly changing and complex operating environments through organizational learning, knowledge management and transformation of organizational norms and values. This is supported by the Fitness Landscape Theory which helps management obtain insights about the interrelationships between internal characteristics (strategy, structure, systems) and external environment. The OD practice stretches beyond the Run The Business (RTB) and the Grow The Business (GTB) service investments and focuses on the Transform The Business (TTB) strategic category of service investments.

Most organizations are in chaos, that is, they are too disorganized and unordered. Organization development theory and practice helps to minimize corporate distress, bankruptcy and failures through enhancing the corporate governance environment of organizations. This is made possible through the organization development's focus on transforming organizations based on adaptation or aligning strategy, structure, processes rewards, and people. These are the five areas that form the Star Model for organization design as developed by Jayr Galbraith. In terms of banking process, the Star Model helps in service design and the development of the service strategy for banks. There are numerous OD concepts that support the development of sound corporate governance:

- *Organizational climate* – this is defined as the mood or unique 'personality' of an organization. Organizational climate features may be associated with employee satisfaction, stress, service quality and outcomes, and successful implementation of new programs. Other characteristics closely related to corporate governance include leadership, participative management, role clarity, and openness of communication. These elements are supported by the concept of industrial democracy and focuses on not only growing but transforming the business. Sound corporate governance should give priority to enhancing organizational climate in order to drive organizational effectiveness.

- *Organizational culture* – this include the deeply seated norms, values, and behaviors that organizational members share. The accelerating pace of change affects these elements of culture and as such demands a new level of adaptability for individuals and organizations. The adoption of OD practices in corporate governance helps in shaping organizational culture and drive organizational effectiveness through encouraging innovation, creativity, informed-risk taking, and suggestions from employees and all other stakeholders.

- *Organizational strategies* – these are the approaches that organizations use in negotiating change. The approaches encompass action research through diagnosis, action planning, interventions and evaluation. In view of complexity science, the organizational strategies should be informed by the methods of optimal solutions such as Decision Support Systems (DSS), Business Intelligence (BI) tools, organizational reengineering and the HR Management Systems. The organizational strategies should be supported by dynamic and agile structure and systems. The organization development strategies should increase an organization's ability to co-adapt, improvise, experimentation and regeneration.

Organization Development is a strategic corporate governance function as it is defined as "an effort that is planned, organization-wide, managed from the top to increase effectiveness and health, through planned interventions in the organization's processes, using behavioral science approaches" – Richard Beckhard, 1969. It is therefore a systematic and holistic approach to aligning strategy, people and processes towards attaining organizational goals and objectives. According to the Institute of Organization Development (IOD), "OD provides organizations with successful change tactics to meet their critical goals while embracing partnerships, collaboration, commitment, accountability, encouragement, and innovation." Based on complexity science theory, demands such skills as design thinking, process visualization and project management. Organization Development helps to resolve diverse organizational issues such as implementing cultural change, determining the mission and values, introducing new systems or processes and enhancing leadership and employee morale. The organization development function is a strategic function that influences the entire organization. The board of directors should view organization development as critical to business success and strategy in order to create great teams and organizations.

Organization Development also attempts to codify structures and processes of organizing. This is supported by the decision engineering framework in order to overcome the *'complexity ceiling'* in solving organization issues. In view of the changing business environment, organization development and corporate governance include widespread learning, engagement and improving organizational functioning thereby enhancing organizational effectiveness. According to Gervase R. Bushe, "Organizational effectiveness requires managing outside and managing inside, having enough stability and having enough flexibility. It requires adapting to external demands and standardizing internal operations. It requires working through people and relationships and working through impersonal processes and routines." These elements demand enhanced corporate governance practices rooted on OD theory and practice, and the application of discovering and prediction techniques. These elements also enhance the fundamental principle of self-organization, that is, the ability of the system to transform itself. Self-organization enables an organization to effectively adapt, evolve; and to be resilient, boundless, and creative.

In view of organizations as complex adaptive systems, bank failure causes can be categorized as resulting from technical problems and adaptive challenges. Technical problems can be solved in a top-down process through the application of analytical models and expertise. Adaptive challenges are complex issues without a single right answer. These problems require inquiry, experimentation, and learning. OD provides a hybrid of assumptions and interventions to deal with both the technical and adaptive challenges in contemporary organizations. Organization Development, as a strategic corporate governance function, seeks to resolve these complex and technical challenges that impact on the efficient and effective function of the entire organization. Organization development research, theory and practice support the principles and practices of corporate governance in the following areas:

- Compensation systems
- Performance monitoring and analysis systems for management and employees
- Employee behavior change
- Determination of KPIs for steering the organization towards its goal
- Leadership, culture and compliance management
- Sustainable consequence management

The adoption of organization development principles helps to ensure organizational agility with respect to globally-active disruptive powers. The organization development function focuses on building the organization's ability to assess its current functioning to achieve its goals and adapt to the ever-changing business environment. The use of Business Intelligence (BI) mechanisms such as scheduled reports, dashboards, trend analysis, forecasting, and Ad-Hoc tools is essential in determining and implementing organizational interventions. These Business Intelligence (BI) mechanisms support the diagnosis and action planning activities of OD. In line with corporate governance frameworks, organization development is oriented to improving the total system, that is, the organization and all its parts based on feedback (information) from both the internal and external environment. Professor Michael Beer defined organization development as "a systematic process of data collection, diagnosis, action planning, intervention, and evaluation aimed at (1) enhancing congruence among organizational structure, process, strategy, people, and culture; (2) developing new and creative organizational solutions; and (3) developing the organization's self-renewing capacity. It occurs through collaboration of organizational members working with a change agent using behavioral science theory, research, and technology."

STRATEGIC IMPORTANCE OF ORGANIZATION DEVELOPMENT

Organization development involves the use of organizational resources to improve efficiency and expand productivity. Besides facilitating culture change, the three main significance of organization development are business growth, improvements in work processes, and enhanced capacity for product innovation.

- *Growth* – OD is an important tool in managing and planning corporate growth. Bank distress and bankruptcy is certain in the event that the business focuses exclusively on the Run The Business (RTB) service investment strategy. OD helps in determining change tactics that support the growth of the business.
- *Work processes* – OD is essential in analyzing work processes for efficiency and accuracy. This is in line with the Grow The Business (GTB) and Transform The Business (TTB) service investment strategy. The focus on resolving technical and adaptive challenges help to build robust business models that sustain the business.
- *Product innovation* – OD helps in the analysis of the different elements of product development or service innovation. OD plays an important role in process management. It helps an

organization devise new ways to manage consumers, change and competition; thereby becoming more efficient and competitive.

REQUIREMENTS FOR EFFECTIVE ORGANIZATION DEVELOPMENT (OD)

- Top management support – the success of OD interventions requires hearted support and approval from the board and executive management. This is because of the strategic thinking and strategic leadership role of top management.
- The organization development interventions should be implemented in consideration of organizational structure. The organization structure should be highly flexible and avoid bureaucratic approaches because such approaches limits the growth and transformation potential of an organization. The board's oversight function is essential in ensuring this alignment between organization development interventions and organizational structure.
- Active participation by supervisors and employees. This is essential in ensuring process and customer focus in service delivery through the development of well-considered and fact-based business strategies.
- Effective communication and feedback system. This is a necessity in order to ensure collaborative working and innovative capacity of work teams and the organization.
- Flexibility – the ever-changing business operating environment requires that organizations effectively adopt change management strategies that respond to the demands of the internal and external environment.
- Data value strategy – banking processes are based on the availability of information and data. A data value strategy helps to enhance the competitive advantage of the firm through leveraging on machine learning, deep learning and cognitive technologies that support company operations. The data value strategy should incorporate data privacy, risk

management and compliance matters. The availability of data helps to make smarter decisions based on facts. Data supports organizational decisions, thereby enabling the organization to accurately define strategy.

The organization development activities are essential to enhancing the corporate governance framework of banking institutions and any other organization through determining effective change tactics that are aligned to the organization's strategic intent. These OD activities can be categorized into three organization development capacities:

- *Technical capacity* – to assist the organization with the core function. This involves the knowledge, training and experience of employees and the systems that an organization has to operationalize the organization's policies and strategies.
- *Advocacy capacity* – ability to communicate and translate strategy. Advocacy capacity is essential in building strong corporate culture that is premised on collaboration and strong partnerships among employees, work teams and strategic business units.
- *Organizational capacity* – the administrative and corporate systems that enable an organization to function more effectively. It involves the organization's capacity to fulfill its mission. This demands strong corporate management and strong corporate governance. Organizational capacity emanates from a strengthened technical and advocacy capacities.

The board of directors, senior executives and managers are responsible for enhancing the capabilities of the organization through the development and implementation of OD interventions in an organization. Organizational capacity is a multi-faceted phenomena and organizations should be seen as working within a living and dynamic system. According to empirical literature, the OD interventions focus on enhancing "the 5Cs" which consist of:

- *The capability to act and commit* – this a measure of the organization's orientation towards 'action'. The capability of an organization to act and commit is a function of the availability of resources; and the overall level of motivation, energy, confidence, volition to move forward, to achieve stated objectives in the face of numerous constraints. This life-given dynamism comes from the quality of corporate governance, quality of decision-making, and the extent of implementing decisions. Organization development (OD) enhances this capacity by enabling the organization's capacity to relate, to maintain coherence and to adapt and renew.

- *The capability to create value* – this capability focuses on creating highly performing organizations based on not only economic results but social and environmental value as well. This capability is a function of the actions, outputs and the relevance and quality of outcomes. The achievement of the capability requires executive support, strategic thinking and operational management.
- *The capability to adapt and self-renew* – the highly volatile and unpredictable business operating environment require organizations adapt and renew themselves in order to remain relevant and sustainable. This demands proactive environmental scanning, adaptive management, imagination, aspiration, rapid learning feedback, and a willingness to innovate by directors, senior executives and managers.
- *The capability to relate to external stakeholders* – to ensure organizational effectiveness, organizations need to effectively relate to all stakeholders. The stakeholder engagement processes of the organization should be enhanced to ensure collaborative action with all stakeholders.
- *The capability to achieve and maintain coherence* – the organization should ensure coherence between the mission, the strategies, resources and actions of the organization. Organization Development (OD) helps to ensure the organization operates as a unified whole, rather than a fragmented collection of loose pieces.

In order to avoid the internal fragmentation of an organization, organization development (OD) aligns strategy, people, and processes thereby releasing the talents and vitality of people in organizations. Boards should adopt the principles and practices of organization development in order to resolve complex issues such as implementing cultural change, determining the organization's mission and values, introducing new systems and processes and enhancing leadership and employee morale. Organization Development is informed by a set of humanistic values and beliefs about the potential of people and organizations. The primary concern of OD is the health and well-being of people at work, and the development and implementation of a strong and dynamic business case. Organization Development leads to organizational effectiveness since it is a democratic and collaborative process that is premised on facts with regards to the business operating environment. OD reflects a shift from the mechanistic view of the firm as it is centered on values of engagement, participation and democracy. The board of directors and all senior leaders in organizations should begin to see OD as a function critical to business success and strategy. OD skills should be among the top priority skills for board of directors, senior leaders and managers of contemporary institutions. The audit unit of the board should incorporate OD diagnostic and audit interventions with a focus on strategy, systems, structures, people, and processes.

Organizational effectiveness is mainly influenced by relationships, people's social needs and motivations and the dynamics of work groups. Board members and senior managers should demonstrate the ability to act as change agents with strong interpersonal skills, relationship building and humanistic values. They should also demonstrate business and strategic awareness and a macro-perspective to corporate management and corporate governance. It is also imperative to have a true appreciation of the value of data and enquiry in driving organizational effectiveness through making fact-based decisions. There are numerous concepts in organization development that should inform corporate governance. These concepts have their roots from Scientific Management, The Hawthorne Studies, and

Bureaucratic Theory Principles. The current OD principles are an improvement of these traditional management principles or studies. Corporate governance frameworks and codes at institutional and national levels need to integrate these evolving contemporary concepts in organization development.

- **Appreciative Inquiry (AI)** – AI is the art and practice of asking questions that focus on strengths, capabilities and the positive potential of the organization. This is based on the assumption that our reality is socially constructed. Board of directors and senior leaders that demonstrate AI are realistic and action-oriented, hence devise innovative ideas for the growth of the business. AI supports the discovery and predictive elements of performance management and measurement because it involves the ability of the board or executives to use generative potential of the business. It is through AI that the requirements for effective organization development bear fruits. Appreciative Inquiry demands a board that is proactive in dealing with challenges and opportunities being brought about by technology. AI helps businesses to understand, address and tackle the changes in business strategy and governance in order to thrive and win.
- **The Burke-Litwin Model** – this is a change model that shows the organization as a system and gives executives insight into the areas of focus for their work. It works as a diagnostic tool to help in determining points of intervention for data gathering, and levers for change. This model revolves around defining and establishing the cause-and-effect relationship between 12 organization dimensions that drive change in organizations. These 12 dimensions are external environment, mission and strategy, leadership, organization culture, structure, systems, management practices, work unit climate, tasks and skills, individual values and needs, motivation level, and individual and overall performance. The board should ensure alignment between these

transformational and transactional organization dynamics in order to effectively manage change.

- **The Emergence Approach** – this model contradicts the rational, deterministic models. The emergence approach suggests that change is inherently unmanageable and as such boards and senior executives cannot hope to control outcomes. Corporate governance should create conditions for change, stimulate progressive conversations and ensure trust or internal credibility.

- **The Real Time Strategic Change** (Jacobs) – this is a methodology for achieving whole system change. It is part of the Large Group Interventions. The approach requires people to share dissatisfaction with the present state and work together to implement the changes required.

- **Systems Thinking** – systems thinking helps to understand the interconnectedness and complexity of organizations, rather than relying on the "linear cause and effect" approaches. It helps in understanding how changing one part of the organization will impact upon the other. This is essential in making informed decisions and also in process mapping and modelling.

- **Learning** – learning at the individual and organizational level is at the heart of change. The works of Kolb on Experiential Learning, Knowles on Adult Learning, and Argyris on Organizational Learning strongly influences training and development design and practice, hence corporate governance. Chapter 11 covers organizational learning as a key method for optimal solutions in contemporary organizations. Action learning approach which is characterized by unending cycle of action, reflection and understanding is key to organizational learning. The action learning framework consisting frame, charge, act, and renew should be adopted in service strategy design at the manufacturing level. Action learning values inclusiveness, participatory approaches and exploration of system dynamics and power relations; hence its role in driving organizational effectiveness.

- **Strategic (transformational) planning** – Strategic planning is essential in ensuring a company makes critical decisions and is the foundation for the firm's operating plans (Boyd, 1991). Transformational planning involves the development of a strategic plan for modifying an enterprise's business processes through the adjustment of policies, procedures and processes to move the organization from an "as is" state to a "to be state" (McIiquaham-Schmidt, 2010).

The following questions are central to the strategic planning process:

- What are the essential practices and procedures for sustainable business operations?
- What are the present and likely future challenges the organization will face?
- How does the organization communicate its mission, vision, strategic goals, and plans to its stakeholders?

Strategic (transformational) planning determines the nature of an organization's corporate governance structure (Boyd, 1991; David, 1997). A firm that has good strategic planning is likely to have effective corporate governance structures. It is extremely important for the board to understand the role of strategic planning in enhancing corporate governance. Its failure can lead to disagreements between the Board and the CEO (Kinross, 2012). Strategic planning is a complex phenomenon conceived of from many complementary aspects. Literature suggests the following dimensions of strategic planning: standardization, sophistication, structure, systemization, severe, superiority, commitment, comprehensiveness, significance, and flexibility of the planning process and programmes (Miller and Cardinal, 1994; Boyd, 1991; Robinson and Pearce, 1988). Effective planning in the banking sector drives organizational effectiveness.

In conclusion, organizations should strive to harness OD theory and practice across all work groups as an imperative for organizational effectiveness. This is because having an integrative and explicit focus on organization development interventions has a tectonic impact on the effectiveness of the entire organization. According to an article by Justine Chinoperekweyi to the Institute of Organization Development (IOD) titled: *'Harnessing OD theory, practice and interventions as a strategic imperative for organizational effectiveness'*, OD theory and practice should be embedded in the modern banking institutions' strategic and operational road maps for the following seven reasons:

- **Fact-based decision making and cultivation of essential leadership traits**

The scale and complexity of the business operating environment require that firms harness OD theory and practice in every fabric of corporate management and governance in order to remain relevant and sustainable. This means organization development should be touted as a strategic imperative for organizational effectiveness. The corporate failures and distress experienced in most economies since the beginning of the century do cast a dark shadow on the exclusive reliance on such skills as economics, finance, banking, accounting and law as defining skills for organizational members. Embedding OD theory and practice in strategic and operational road maps is vital in ensuring fact-based decision-making and the cultivation of essential leadership traits such as mission focused, visionary, analytical, and objectivity among work group members. These leadership traits improve strategic thinking and strategic leadership across work groups. The OD theory and practice is instrumental in reinforcing the leaders' capacity to provide necessary advice and counsel, and improve organizational legitimacy and sustainability.

- **Minimize risks by addressing the increasing digital complexities**

The increasing digital complexities in the business operating environment necessitate the need for organizational change strategies rooted on OD theory and practices. Harnessing OD theory and practice inside and outside the board room is essential in expanding knowledge; enhancing organizational climate, organizational structure, and organizational strategies. Organizations that prioritize and cultivate OD skills across work groups have an improved capacity for solving organizational problems, managing change, and achieve internal coherence that gives significant competitive advantages to the firm.

- **Aligning an organization to the operating environment**

Without downgrading the other skills required of directors and other organizational members as specified in various codes and policies in different jurisdictions, OD is a strategic imperative for organizational effectiveness because of its focus on aligning organizations with the rapidly changing and complex operating environment. Harnessing OD theory and practice across work groups enhances organizational learning, knowledge management, adaptive management and the transformation of organizational norms and values. OD is instrumental in organizational effectiveness because it helps directors and senior executives devise change management tactics that strategically reposition the business in an evolving environment while embracing partnerships, collaboration and innovation.

- **Enhancing the capacity to resolve complex emergent issues**

Organizations that consider OD as a strategic imperative have the capacity to resolve complex organizational issues such as cultural change, introducing new systems or processes, determining the organization's mission and values, and enhancing leadership and employee engagement. The field of OD is critical to business success and strategy through widespread learning, engagement and constant inquiry that enhances the organization's capacity to deal with prevalent mega-disruptions, and thrive. It also supports the application of discovery and prediction techniques to further the achievement of organizational goals. Due to the volatility, ambiguity and unpredictability of the business environment, organizations encounter technical and adaptive challenges that require the proactive adoption and application of analytical models and expertise. The models and expertise that drive effectiveness at board and organizational level require harnessing the theory and practices of OD as developed through inquiry, experimentation and learning. The hybrid interventions that OD bring to corporate board rooms enable organizations to be responsive to trends, opportunities, shocks and pressures, and to resolve the complex and disruptive technical and adaptive challenges in organizational life.

- **Building congruence across the entire organization**

The process of harnessing OD theory and practice supports organizational effectiveness in the following areas: compensation systems, performance measurement and management, sustainable consequences management, leadership and culture change and so on. It also ensures the building of congruence among the organizational structure, process, strategy, people and culture. The ensuing congruence leads to enhanced competitive advantage as a result of sustained business growth, improvements in work processes, and enhanced capacity to innovate and self-renew. OD helps the board to manage risks and to devise innovate ways of managing consumers/customers, change and competition.

- **Unifying people in organizations**

OD theory, practice and interventions unifies the board, C-suites, managers and all other work groups thereby contributing to the development and effective implementation of well-considered and fact-based business strategies. It significantly influences and alters relationships and motivation of not only board members but the dynamics of all work groups that characterize the entire organization. OD is not normative and therefore promotes systems thinking which helps to understand the interconnectedness and complexity of organizations.

- **Increasing strategic awareness among all members**

Embedding OD theory and practice in the board room is the inevitable catalyst to addressing all business challenges through enhanced strategic awareness and macro-perspective to corporate governance, which leads to the organization's capacity to thrive and win. OD skills training and education should be a top priority on director continuous capacity development programmes of the modern corporation. Organizations should seriously consider enhancing the organization development skills of all members in order to build high performing teams, improve individual capabilities, create an enabling environment, and improve organizational performance.

OD is not a normative field; however, for organizations to optimize on the benefits of harnessing its theory and practice as operational and strategic imperatives the seven areas below should be the focus of attention. The capacity and professional development programmes for directors, C-suites, managers and other work groups should:

- Promote the use of Decision Support Systems and Business Intelligence (BI) tools across all work groups. This requires the definition of the organization's data value strategy.
- Encourage the development and implementation of structured and integrative risk governance framework coupled with strategic (transformational) planning.
- Promote enlightened environmental scanning and action learning methodologies.
- Promote strategic alignment through process-oriented organizational reengineering methodologies.
- Promote management innovation through R&D across work teams in order to develop well-honed product and service innovations.
- Devise an integrated Human Resource Management System that unifies all members of the organization.
- Devise a Performance Management System that is integrative and focuses all members on a common objective.

CHAPTER 10

SPIRITUALITY AND BUSINESS ETHICS IN CORPORATE GOVERNANCE

This chapter reviews the role of spirituality and business ethics in improving corporate governance in the banking sector. Spirituality and business ethics are essential practices in minimizing the agency problem through addressing issues of adverse selection and moral hazards among corporate players. This view contradicts the Scientific Management principles and principles of the Bureaucratic Theory that focuses on the mechanistic view of the firm. People are at the center of the service industry, hence the need to adopt behavioral science methodologies to address organizational issues.

THE MECHANISTIC VERSUS THE ORGANISTIC VIEW OF THE ORGANIZATION

The study of organizations has undergone a fundamental shift from a Newtonian paradigm (mechanistic) that values reason and scientific principles to a spiritual paradigm (organistic) that values consciousness and understanding (Whitty, 1997). This shift necessitated the movement from reductive analysis and reliance on predetermined plans to more holistic analyses of organizational life. The mechanistic view states that individuals can be scientifically measured and categorized based on intellectual and other characteristics they possess, and that certain people are meant to be leaders whereas others are meant to be mere followers. This view places greater reliance on rational laws that dictate the only correct way of doing things. This view also has a strong belief in scarcity of resources leading to practices such as "antagonism, political manipulation, 'padding' of budget requests, empire building, and lack of trust and cooperation between persons and organizational units" (Whitty, 1997).

The agency theory is founded on the mechanistic view and the principles of Scientific Management as developed by Frederick Taylor. In line with Max Weber's Bureaucratic Theory, corporate governance under the mechanistic paradigm focuses on the establishment of specific procedures and rules of behavior; hence the organizations are characterized by rigid, bureaucratic structures and hierarchical chains of command. In line with Scientific Management principles and the Bureaucratic Theory, organizations under the mechanistic view make use of formal communication channels, very formal procedures manuals and policy manuals. The governance framework in this case relies on the use of incentives and supervision to address the agency problem. Organizations that follow the mechanistic paradigm make use of Policy Making boards and are characterized by the dominance of controlling shareholders.

The mechanistic paradigm to corporate governance view corporate executives as atomic self-interest driven individuals with little regard for achieving organizational objectives. This view is aligned to the McGregor Theory X which state that people are inherently lazy, need to be controlled and coerced to work, avoid personal responsibility and opportunities for stretch and are only concerned with their own safety and security needs. Due to this negative agency problem, the mechanistic paradigm necessitated the exponential increase in the number of laws, regulations and guidelines directed at organizations. Legal reforms are regarded as the only solution to corporate challenges under the mechanistic paradigm. The mechanistic view believes that corporate distress, collapse and scandals are inevitable in the absence of regulations, policies and procedures. Most of the existing corporate governance regulations and codes are based entirely on the mechanistic paradigm, and the negative agency problem.

Organizations are extremely complex and as such a non-linear approach to governance should be adopted. The characteristics of complex systems necessitate the need for models based on non-linear approach to reality. This is because of the following features of complex systems:

- Complex systems cannot be managed and directed by means of reductionism, i.e. by splitting the whole into component parts and adding them up, as they are made up of elements that make sense only within the integrity of the system;
- Complex systems evolve unpredictably and as such are uncontrollable and disordered;
- Complex systems can undergo sudden changes in state (bifurcations);
- Complex systems have autopoietic (self-organizing) capacity;
- Complex systems are characterized by evolution and dynamics.

The mechanistic approach follows a linear approach and as such cannot be effective in complex systems. There is therefore a need to adopt the spiritual paradigm to corporate governance in order to address such features of the modern dynamic organizations as non-linearity, emergence, self-organizing, and nested systems. The spiritual paradigm brings about positive corporate governance perspective, which is a radical departure from the "anti-management" approach exhibited in the rules and codes-based corporate governance frameworks. This approach recognizes the positive strengths and virtues of corporate executives. Organizations that adopt the spiritual paradigm focus on fostering a positive corporate culture and developing and enhancing the positive virtues of managers and executives thereby resolving complexity issues. The spiritual paradigm indicates that managers are open to change and they work in concert with teams to accomplish mutual objectives. The existence of the abundance mentality among the principals and agents leads to the adoption of the win-win strategies in conflict resolution hence greater interconnectedness, cooperation and employee empowerment. These elements support adaptation and co-evolution of organizations.

"Spirituality and management, once thought incompatible have in the past decade fallen in love" (Benefiel, 2003). Spirituality is the basis for evolutionary and revolutionary corporate governance, as a result of the need and emphasis of envisioning the future and adopting change management methodologies in the modern corporation. Most of these change management methodologies fall under the Business Process Reengineering (BPR) and focus on Transform The Business (TTB) service investments. There has been an increased interest in workplace spirituality and its role in corporate governance and organizational effectiveness because of the increased rate of corporate greed and collapses; and the understanding among organizations that corporate governance and corporate management are behavioral issues and as such require the adoption of behavioral science approaches to ensure positive results. There is an exponential increase in human gluttony and lack of love and compassion in the corporate world due to the pursuit of self-centered interests which leads to increased agency costs. The bank failure case studies profiled in the introductory chapter of this book points out to the weaknesses of the mechanistic paradigm that triggered in humankind a renewed search for harmony and peace, hence the spiritual progress in the corporate world. Spirituality and business ethics emphasizes teamwork, trust, creativity and openness to change as approaches to enhancing corporate governance and organizational effectiveness. The adoption of the spiritual paradigm signifies the shift from the shareholder to the stakeholder view of the firm. This is supported by the action learning methodology which values inclusiveness, participatory approaches and exploration of system dynamics and power relations in order to drive organizational effectiveness.

Dynamic organizations such as banks need to take advantage of subjective thinking features such as process-oriented thinking, creative thinking, causal thinking, Holism, system thinking, strategic thinking, inductive and deductive thinking, intuitive thinking, and dynamic thinking. These features address the mechanistic paradigm which promotes narrow thinking, dogmatism, individual orienting, and linear thinking.

IMPORTANCE OF SPIRITUALITY AND BUSINESS ETHICS IN BANKING OPERATIONS

A consideration of spirituality and business ethics in corporate governance is a strategic imperative because workplace spirituality is regarded as "a sanctified and blessed intangible asset for an organizational long-term progress and survival" (Danish, 2010). This is primarily because "the wisdom of the Scriptures enlightens the moral understanding of market fragilities and renews a commitment of the faithful toward behaviour that pleases God rather than man" (Smith, 2010). The executionary behaviour of corporate executives and the prime focus on determining economic solutions while the religious problem is ignored or held in suspense; is considered as the main problem in organizational life. It is this ignorance of the spiritual paradigm that perpetuates the agency problem in contemporary organizations despite the increased attention being given to sound corporate governance principles and practices. In order to achieve and sustain organizational effectiveness, organizations should openly incorporate the principles of workplace spirituality in their business models. The exclusive focus on economic solutions by corporate governance players should be avoided and organizations should fulfill all the four responsibilities or the "four faces" of the corporation: economic, legal, ethical, and philanthropic (Carroll, 2000). These responsibilities should form part of the performance management dashboard of contemporary organizations. "Ethics have come to be on par with economics as the primary criterion for evaluating corporate performance, not because economic value has become less important, but because it is taken for granted, and ethical performance is not" (Wilson, 2000). Corporate directors, executives and managers need to appreciate that the reliance on analyzing market-based and accounting indicators of performance does not amount to an effective strategy for banks. This is because the performance of banks interlinks both economic and non-financial indicators (Sagar and Rajesh, 2008).

BUILDING A SPIRITUAL ORGANIZATION

Organizations should reflect the spiritual paradigm through spiritual values that form part of the organization's culture and these values should inform behaviour, decision-making, and resource allocation. Spirituality should be encouraged at the individual, team and organizational levels in order to avoid the agency problem as was the case in the profiled bank failure case studies. Employees should be encouraged to willingly participate in spiritual values to modify organizational planning and strategy making, human resource management practices, and building a culture that provides a context for daily life. The development and implementation of a holistic and robust HR Management Support System is essential in building spiritual organizations. Empirical literature indicates that spiritual organizations in line with the positive governance principles have the following five characteristics:

- Strong sense of purpose in work
- Prioritizes individual development
- Focus on building trust and openness within the entire organization
- Empowerment of all employees
- Employee expression is greatly tolerated

The key practices of spiritual organizations that banks should adopt include career counseling, meditation centers, work-life balance, prayer groups, healthy work environment, ethics and core values, programs that integrate work and family, servant leadership and stewardship. These practices should be incorporated in the HR Management Support System. Boards that prioritize spiritual and ethical values in their operations build sustainable organizations. This is because spiritual and ethical values lead to increased productivity, profitability, employee retention, customer loyalty, and brand reputation. Prioritizing employees' spirituality leads to a reduction in stress levels, enhanced employee creativity and improved problem-solving. This can be achieved if the board, senior leaders and managers effectively play their roles of enabling, synergizing, and providing super-ordination.

Spiritual and ethical values lead to engaged, committed and innovative workforce. Engaged and committed employees, through their discretionary effort give their organizations a crucial competitive advantage, plus productivity and lower staff-turnover. In view of the significant role of spirituality in organizational life, corporate executives in banking should broaden their problem-solving and decision-making approaches to incorporate spiritual dimensions. The decision reengineering techniques should incorporate the spiritual paradigm of decision making. Corporate governance is a behavioral issue and as such requires spiritual principles in order to ensure effectiveness. Cuba *et al.,* (2006) state that "Spirituality at organizational level imbues organizational structures with spiritual qualities that drive effectiveness."

The characteristics of spiritual organizations can be equated to Theory Z of Ouchi by Dr. William Ouchi. The characteristics of Theory Z organization include long-term employment, participative decision-making processes, company specific skills and its broad concern for employees and working relationships. In sharp contrast to the agency theory, this Japanese consensus management style assumes that employees want to build cooperative relationships with their employers, peers, and that they have well-developed sense of dedication, moral obligations, and self-discipline. This positive view to corporate governance is also supported by McGregor Theory Y. Theory Y contradicts the agency view and the mechanistic view and state that people enjoy work, can be self-directed in pursuit of agreed objectives; accept and seek responsibility and have a capacity for solving organizational problems when provided with the right organizational environment. These views are aligned with the principles of Organization Development (OD) and are in sharp contrast to the mechanistic paradigm of corporate governance.

CHAPTER 11

CORPORATE MEETINGS

Corporations have assumed a dominant position in the 21st century society; and organizational effectiveness is undoubtedly a key pillar to economic transformation. The dominance of the corporation can be measured by the number of corporate entities, employment levels, economic growth in different countries, the pace of technological innovations, and the extent of social impact by corporate entities. The corporation, particularly banks, is the main form of corporate activity in any country. In the modern corporation, meetings are an essential instrument for enhancing organizational effectiveness. The effectiveness and alignment of all corporate meetings determines an organization's overall effectiveness and subsequently economic performance. From the vantage point of the stakeholder theory, the outcomes of any organization's meeting have significant implications on different stakeholders and the whole corporate ecosystem. This is equally important for banks in view of the globalization of markets and the role of the banking sector in an economy.

The science of corporate meetings has assumed increased academic interest (Allen *et al.*, 2008) due to increases in corporate scandals, increased corporate failures, rapid and disruptive changes in the business environment, growth in conglomerate structures, increased competition, and reduced product lifecycles. These factors therefore call for an extensive inquiry into the alignment of corporate meetings in order to drive organizational effectiveness through participatory and collaborative approaches. In view of the complexity of the

21st century business environment, the importance of corporate meetings in accomplishing organizational work cannot be overemphasized (Rogelberg *et al.*, 2010). Corporate meetings enable the collective accomplishment of organizational tasks by individuals and teams (Romano and Nunamaker Jr, 2001). It is important for organizations to continually strive to increase the effectiveness of corporate meetings because prior research showed that ineffective meetings are likely to have lasting psychological effects on employees (Nixon and Littlepage, 1992). Corporate meetings are "microcosms for the entire organization where the power, structure, and functions of the organization is manifested, legitimized and perpetuated" (Schwartzman, 1986).

An organization is a social unit of people that is structured in order to pursue collective goals. Theorists of formal organization state that organizations have objectives (Fayol, 1949) and purposes (Urwick, 1943). The effectiveness of an organization is influenced by decisions from within and from outside the formal structure. *Can an organization operate effectively without integrated, organized, and effective meetings?* Meetings are an integral and pervasive part of any social construction. People in organizations meet to generate ideas (Reinig and Shin, 2003), solve organization's problems (Romano and Nunamaker Jr, 2001; McComas *et al.*, 2007), share information (Vree, 2011), socialization (Horan, 2012), shaping an organization's culture, relationship building, and training (Clark, 1998). Organizations also use meetings as forums to communicate the organization's strategic intent, craft strategic plans, and develop responses to environmental changes. Organizational effectiveness refers to efficiency within which an organization achieves its objectives. Meetings and meetings integration are essential corporate governance instruments in strategic alignment and subsequently organizational effectiveness.

This chapter focuses on the strategic role of meetings as instruments for organizational effectiveness. This exploration covers six categories of meetings in terms of their essential ingredients, incentives for effectiveness, and the interface of these meetings in order to create alignment of the different units of the organization, streamline each unit and enhance innovation for organizational effectiveness. The six categories of meetings that form part of this exploration are the General Shareholder Meeting (GSM), Board meetings, Executive Committee meetings, Management meetings, Stakeholder engagement meetings, and Staff meetings. The formal and informal meeting styles are essential in ensuring the integration of meetings in any organization. Though on the surface an organization presents a single entity, the hierarchical view of an organization is considered in the categorization of corporate meetings. An organization has boundaries, levels, operating controls and authorities. However, the context of meetings actually varies depending on the subcultures of which the employee belongs in the organization, subcultures defined by such things as organizational rank and orientation, job functions, educational level, length of employment, age and so on (Kramer, 2001). The alignment of the six meetings and the harmonious interaction between all members of these distinct categories of meetings is fundamental determining and sustaining optimal solutions for the organization.

As shown in Chapter 7, the hierarchical view of the organization considers three main levels of an organization: lower level, middle level, and top-level management. The focus of each level in view of organizational effectiveness varies from operational to strategic as one moves up the organization's hierarchy. Each level forms part of the total organization, hence the necessity of ensuring meetings alignment at each level in view of driving sustained organizational effectiveness.

Each level of the organization provides strategic support to the other levels in order to perform the core work of the organization. However, the skills, structure, processes and systems required to conduct effective meetings at each level varies. There seem to be significant variations in terms of the incentives of corporate meetings at different functional levels of an organization. It is therefore important to examine the form and essence of the different categories of corporate meetings in relation to sustainable organizational effectiveness.

Corporate meetings should be aligned and there should be harmonious interaction between all members at different levels of the organization. Synergy, adaptation, goal-orientation and coordinated balance are essential to sustainable organizational effectiveness. Meetings alignment is therefore essential to ensure streamlined and innovative activities at each level of the organization.

MEANING OF MEETINGS AND THEIR IMPORTANCE

Corporate meetings play an integral role in an organization. An organization cannot function effectively without engaging in effective corporate meetings. Meetings provide all corporate stakeholders with an opportunity to communicate and coordinate the strategic intent of the organization (Rogelberg *et al.*, 2006). Corporate meetings are the engines for a multitude of organizational activities, from problem solving to interactions between different organizational functions. The process of defining meetings is at the centre of meeting sciences because an accurate definition of meetings reveals the purposes and the specific techniques required for each meeting to be effective. There is no consensus among corporate meeting scholars and researchers on the exact definition of meetings. According to Schwartzman (1986) meetings represent any form of pre-arranged, work-related gatherings and interaction between two or more individuals. Consistently, and more recently, Rogelberg *et al.*, (2006) defined meetings as "purposeful work-related interactions occurring between at least two individuals that have more structure than a simple chat, but less than a lecture." "A meeting is a gathering where people speak up, say nothing, and then disagree" (Kayser, 1990). According to Nunamaker *et al.*, (1991) a meeting is "any activity where people come together, whether at the same place at the same time, or in different places at different time." Van Vree (2011) corroborated on the definition of meetings by Boden (1994) which state that meetings refer to the social action through which members of an organizational produce and reproduce the organization's strategic intent.

MEETINGS STYLES

Literature on the typologies of meeting types and meeting purposes is relatively scant. Schwartzman (1986) described the first typology of meetings which encompass scheduled or unscheduled (Schwartzman, 1986). The difference between these two is the time spent on planning or preparing for the meeting. Most of the current research focuses on the regularly scheduled, formal meetings rather that the highly marginalized unscheduled meetings (Rogelberg *et al.,* 2006). The meetings typology by Schwartzman (1986) can be summarized as an early attempt to categorize meetings and provide a means for differentiating between formal versus informal meeting settings. Another typology of meetings was developed by Bilbow (2002). This typology distinguishes between cross-departmental meetings, weekly departmental meetings, and brainstorming meetings. These different meetings fall under the "scheduled" meeting category by Schwartzman (1986). Therefore, meetings can generally be categorized as formal and informal meetings. The interaction between these two categories of meetings styles is essential for organizational effectiveness in the banking industry.

TYPES OF MEETINGS

Corporate meetings provide huge value to companies, employees, and the wider society (Boden, 1994). This value is in the form of shareholder wealth maximization, stakeholder value or shared value, and embedded sustainability. The six general types of meetings in modern organizations are: "Status Update Meetings, Information Sharing Meetings, Decision Making Meetings, Problem Solving Meetings, Innovation Meetings, and Team Building Meetings" (Boden, 1994). In addressing these six types of meetings, this section reviews meetings from a hierarchical perspective of the organization.

STAFF MEETINGS/TEAM MEETINGS

These are meetings that are typically called by a team leader or manager to direct or indirect subordinates. Staff motivation is paramount to 21st century leadership and management. Organizations use energized staff meetings as an effective way to motivate staff (Eller and Eller, 2006). Staff meetings are a useful and powerful instrument for organizational development, for the sharing of views (Van Vree, 2011), and for decision making (Reinig and Shin, 2003). The key problems affecting the alignment of staff meetings include lack of charter, lack of clarity, and staff uncertainty (Topman, 1996). The staff meeting is the most effective way through which managers communicate objectives (Rogelberg *et al.*, 2010). Staff meetings are useful to chart progress and keep staff informed of all office activities. "The interaction of many minds is usually more illuminating than the intuition of one" – Theodore C. Sorensen. Staff meetings are generally an important part of communication in the workplace. Corporate meetings represent the general mode for staff to share information, discuss work-related challenges and opportunities, and make corporate decisions (Boden, 1994). Corporate managers and leaders prioritize meetings as a strategic activity because meetings encourage discussion and yields optimal solutions for the organization. Staff meetings encourage two-way communication and are often used to pull together information for decision making, communicating problems or solutions, and provide focus for teams (Masters and Wallace, 2011). The promotion of two-way communication is an essential element of the integration process and mutual decision making.

MANAGEMENT MEETINGS

Chapter 7 covered the role of managers in corporate governance and the need for middle management revolution. Management meetings are crucial in driving the middle management revolution and in developing and implementing Organization Development (OD) interventions. Management meetings refer to meetings at which management or administrative employees from various levels in the organization gather to report on their areas of responsibility and learn about new policies, procedures, and challenges. Management meetings should be held on a regular basis. Management meetings mainly save to secure corporate wealth maximization, coupled with the maximum prosperity for individual employees. The words "maximum prosperity" does not give exclusive focus to shareholder wealth maximization, but the expansion, development, and transformation of every unit and function of the business to its highest state of excellence. This is important in ensuring sustained prosperity for the employer and for each employee. Maximum prosperity for individual employees encompasses the growth of each employee to a state of maximum efficiency. This is essential in ensuring the employees can perform to the best of their natural abilities. Scientific management supports the view that the long-term prosperity of the employer can only be achieved and sustained if accompanied by the prosperity of each employee, and vice-versa. The close, intimate, personal cooperation between employers and employees is of the essence of modern scientific management (Taylor, 2008). Management meetings are instrumental is ensuring this close cooperation and supporting the supervisory board in a two-tier board system.

According to the University of Manitoba (2014) the functions of management meetings are important for the following reasons:

- Make decisions at an operational level, consistent with the strategic intent
- Operationalize and monitor progress toward the achievement of strategic goals
- Suggest policy changes
- Review requests and decisions by departmental units
- Develop departmental budgets based on departmental priorities

The basic functions of management are useful in determining the importance of meetings. As reviewed in Chapter 7, these functions are planning, organizing, leading, controlling, and coordination.

Management controls aims at transforming firm boundaries and sustaining hybrid organizations to mitigate risk and facilitate collaboration in intra-firm transactions. Management meetings are essential in facilitating coordination in intra-firm transactions (Shannon and Dekker, 2014).

EXECUTIVE COMMITTEE MEETINGS

The executive committee is more of a smaller board and as such should function more like a board than an actual committee. The executive committee plays an important role in recommending strategic policy and priorities, governance policy and structure, financial planning, fiscal policy, and human resources and labor relations. The reports generated from the executive committee meeting forms the basis of the board meeting and GSM. The focus of the executive committee meeting is to ensure the proper functioning of the organization and make strategic decisions. The executive committee meetings should be held prior to and just after the board meetings and the GSM. The significance of the executive committee meetings can be reviewed in the context of the functions of the committee. These functions include: driving the management's agenda, reviewing the company's performance, reviewing corporate strategy and risks, setting operations and financial objectives, structuring and managing internal business controls, corporate social responsibility issues, and review of compliance with applicable laws and regulations (Shannon and Dekker, 2014). The committee provides guidance and leadership to the overall organization's work and enhances the effectiveness of the board.

BOARD OF DIRECTORS' MEETINGS

These are meetings held at definite intervals and for administrative purposes. Strategic decision making is central to organizational effectiveness. Strategic decisions include infrequent decisions taken by top management of the firm. These decisions have a direct bearing on a firm's survival and health. A board is reckoned as "a team brought together to work towards achieving organizational goals" (Langton and Robbins, 2007). The difference between the board and executives or management is that executives and management are in the organization's chain of command whilst directors are not in the chain of command but are there to provide technical service to it. Boards have a crucial responsibility towards strategy and organizational effectiveness, hence the importance of board meetings. A large body of board and governance literature has now been published because companies are a legal construction that has a dominant role in society. The increase in reports of moral failures, hubris, incompetence, judicial investigations and sanctions published in popular press and practitioner literature have heightened awareness amongst a broad constituency. The objective of much of the body of research published to date has been the discovery of the optimal board configuration through which to minimize a perceived agency problem thought to exist between the board and management (Chandler, 1962).

As elaborated in Chapter 3, the significance of board meetings as instruments for strategic alignment, corporate sustainability and profitability can be determined by reviewing the roles of the board. Board meetings are essential for strategic management, especially strategy development, strategic decision-making and monitoring of strategy implementation. The responsibility for the performance of the limited liability firm lies with the board (Cadburry, 1997). Board meetings are important in enhancing the oversight function of the board. Letende (2004) pointed out that boards should regularly review the performance of management and the performance of the firm. Board meetings therefore enhance the monitoring of management, resulting in improved corporate performance. Directors use the board meeting as a platform to develop the mission of the organization (Bart and Bonits, 2003), setting and reviewing the organization's mission (Walker, 1999), and implementing strategic initiatives in the context of predefined corporate objectives.

Board meetings also provide a platform for directors to engage in strategic thinking (Garrett, 1996), and strategic leadership (Davies, 1999). "Strategic thinking is related to long-term organizational effectiveness and involves strategic analysis, strategy formulation and corporate direction" (Garrett, 1996). Strategic leadership is a balance of strategic skills and experience relative to the organization's strategic intent. The top responsibility for board meetings includes the establishment of the firm's policy/vision, financial analysis and performance monitoring, and supporting strategies to achieve competitive advantage (Van der Walt and Ingley, 2001). A study in Australia identified "strategy formulation, strategic decision-making and strategic control" (Kemp, 2006) as the reasons for board meetings. According to Wheeler and Hunger (2004), the board meetings should focus on monitoring the market and performance to keep abreast of competitors; evaluating, influencing and examining management proposals, decisions, and actions; and initiate and determine the organization's mission and specify strategic options to management. According to Tricker (1984) the board functions include establishing the vision, overseeing corporate strategy, assessing and monitoring performance. The board meetings are also useful for examining alternative business opportunities (Coulson-Thomas, 1993).

Board meetings should focus on key organizational and managerial levers in order to expedite ambitious growth strategies (Penrose, 1959). The cognition lever is a key governance lever to influence managerial decision-making (Witz, 2011). 'Relationship' is also an important factor in supporting and sustaining growth (Anderson and Reeb, 2003). This is because an organization is a social construction whose functioning is greatly influenced by relationships. The disciplinary lever focuses on monitoring and control (Chandler, 1991).

Organizations also use board meetings to determine the intensity of board activity and value relevant board attribute (Vafeas, 1999). Despite the benefits associated with board meetings, there are significant costs involved such as: managerial time, travel expenses, and directors' fees (Vafeas, 1999). The number of board meetings also has significant implications of the quality of audit (Carcello *et al.,* 2002). This assertion implies that a higher quality audit work protects the shareholders' interest and improves firm performance. According to Lipton and Lorsch (1992) and Jensen (1993), "board meetings are not necessarily useful because, given the limited time available they cannot be used for meaningful exchange of ideas among directors."

GENERAL SHAREHOLDER MEETINGS (GSM)

This category of meetings is granted high legal importance in all jurisdictions. This follows the view that "shareholders, as suppliers of finance to the companies, are in need of mechanisms to ensure positive returns on their investments" (Shleifer and Vishny, 1997). The significance of annual general meetings was published by the European Commission published a 2011 green paper. The green paper highlighted the importance of annual general meetings as instruments to achieve long-term sustainable returns in the corporate sector. Most of the European national corporate governance codes also emphasize on the importance of general meetings (de Jong *et al.,* 2006).

The GSM is a mandatory yearly meeting of the general membership of an organization. The meeting represents all shareholders and the shareholders exercise all the rights that correspond to the company. The three types of general shareholder meetings are ordinary, universal, and extraordinary. "General meetings first appear as initial attempts to practice local democracy in the twelfth century" (O'Donnell, 1952). In Switzerland, for example, townsfolk gathered to vote for a number of agenda items once a year (Cordery, 2005), and the early parish structure in Great Britain contained yearly general meetings to vote for top officials in a local governance system (Cordery, 2005). There is an increasing body of literature that emphasizes the shareholders' need to monitor management (Shleifer and Vishny, 1986; Maug, 1998). The classical theoretical dilemmas surrounding the power between owners and managers in terms of ownership separation necessitate the importance of the annual general meetings. Annual General Meetings are an active response to the agency problem (Berle and Means, 1932). The annual general meetings are therefore historically founded as mechanisms to regulate agency relationships (Cordery, 2005). Shareholders utilize the GSM as a forum to exercise their right to vote, which is a mode of decision-taking by a plurality of people. Voting rights complement and compensate shareholders for incomplete contracts (Baums, 2000), and thus, constitute an important part of the share value (Amzaleg *et al.*, 2005).

The legal explanations of annual general meetings vary across jurisdictions (Baums, 2000). In Germany, the general meeting focuses on a limited number of corporate issues. On the other hand, general meetings in Zimbabwe are the ultimate decision-making body. The purposed of holding general meetings range from agency perspectives. The general meeting has been considered a "key mechanism for promoting transparency and accountability in the management of company" (Company Law Review Steering Group, 1999). General meetings are to be seen as "rituals" and the main purpose is to maintain the organization's status quo (Hodges *et al.*, 2004). General meetings are aimed to "make important business decisions, monitor internally appointed directors, and provide advice to management" (Iwantani and Taki, 2009). In general, the GSM provides a platform for directors to exercise of corporate democracy, assess the performance of managers, and collectively deliberate on strategic issues affecting the business by shareholders (Sjostrom, 2006).

Startling (2003) indicates that general meetings help in regulating agency relationships through providing shareholders with information on financial performance of the firm. The transfer of corporate information from the management to shareholders is crucial in enhancing corporate decision making, evaluating the performance of management and the board, and hold managers to account of their actions. Organizations also use the general as a forum where directors can gain shareholder consent for decisions outside managerial discretion. The general meeting also offers an opportunity for interaction of shareholders on pertinent issues about the growth of the business. Shareholder proposals and proxy voting are the primary tools for corporate investors to attempt to affect corporate decision-making (Gillan and Starks, 1998). Yermack (2010) concludes that "shareholders use voting as a channel of communication with board of directors, and protest voting can lead to significant changes in corporate governance and strategy" (Yermack, 2010). Shareholders also has an opportunity to exercise 'voice', defined as attempts to affect a change in the state of affairs "through individual or collective petition to the management directly in charge or through various types of actions and protests, including those that are meant to mobilize public opinion" (Hirschman, 1970). This includes face-to-face communication with management and other stakeholders. Gray *et al.,* (1988) state that general meetings function as a counterweight to managerial priority of major shareholders since all shareholders are given the right to question management. This opportunity to question management on pertinent business issues represents a valuable accountability mechanism (Cordery, 2005).

STAKEHOLDER ENGAGEMENT MEETINGS

A stakeholder refers to any individual or group who has a vested interest in the outcome of an organization's actions. Stakeholders can be divided into internal and external stakeholders. Internal stakeholders represent individuals who are already committed to serving an organization. Examples of internal stakeholders are staff, executive leadership, and board members. External stakeholders represent individuals who are impacted by an organization's work as service recipients. Examples include customers, competitors, community members, government, funders, and advocacy/interest groups. According to Freeman (1984) the definition of stakeholders can either be "narrow" or "broad". The narrow definition encompasses groups which are vital to the survival and success of an organization. The broad view includes "individuals and organisations that affect or are affected by the activities of an organisation" (Freeman, 1984). Mitchell *et al.,* (1997) indicated power, legitimacy and urgency as the three important relationship attributes useful for classification of stakeholders.

According to Clarkson (1995), stakeholders can be classified as primary and secondary stakeholders. Primary stakeholders encompass individuals vital for the survival of the organization. The level of interdependence is high on primary stakeholders as compared to secondary stakeholders. Secondary stakeholders are those who affect or are affected by the organization, but without direct interaction with the organization. The organization does not necessarily depend on secondary stakeholders but sometimes can have negative impact on business (Clarkson, 1995).

The engagement of stakeholders is an essential and mutually beneficial strategic function that results in organizational effectiveness. Stakeholder engagement meetings are crucial for enhanced collaboration and shared decision-making. The four levels of stakeholder engagement are: inform, consult, involve, and collaborate/empower (DCFS, 2013). There is no common understanding on the meaning and characteristics of effective stakeholder engagement (Sloan, 2009). Greenwood (2007) purports that stakeholder thinking and stakeholder engagement areas are under-theorized. Stakeholder engagement is one of the several principles "to successfully create, trade and sustain value" (Freeman *et al.*, 2007). Effective organizations view stakeholders as active collaborators and partners to create sustainable opportunities (Sloan, 2009). "Stakeholder thinking is about being interactive, mutually-engaged and responsive with stakeholders in doing business, thus building the foundation for transparency and accountability. It serves to understand and remedy the business problems of creating values, connecting capitalism with ethics and helping management development to address the corporate problems" (Parmar *et al.*, 2010). Unlike the shareholder perspective, stakeholder engagement takes into account all the company's stakeholders (Freeman *et al.*, 2007; Kakabadse *et al.*, 2005).

In support of stakeholder dialogue and stakeholder knowledge integration, Ayuso *et al.,* (2006) pointed out that "stakeholder dialogue leverages organizational resources that promote two-way communication, transparency and appropriate feedback to stakeholders; stakeholder knowledge integration relies on non-hierarchical structures, flexibility and openness to change." The literature on stakeholder engagement mechanisms is relatively scant; as such the definition and mechanisms of stakeholder engagement vary among different organization.

CHAPTER 12

METHODS OF OPTIMAL SOLUTIONS

The introduction chapter of this book profiled six examples of bank failures in different countries. The profiled case studies illustrated varied corporate governance deficiencies in the way banks were or are being directed and managed. Though bank failures are inevitable in any economy, most bank failures advertise lack of effective internal controls, the folly of trusting one employee, lack of board oversight, shareholder domination, poor risk management, compensation systems that exclusively focus on rewarding external competencies, 'corporate incest', lack of employee engagement and significant corporate reporting deficiencies. Due to the complexity of corporate governance and the rising volatility of the business environment, there is an urgent need for banks to develop and implement methods of optimal solutions in the banking services sector in order to ensure sector stability and solvency. The uniqueness of banks demands that the manner in which banks are managed and directed be considered a top priority in economic management. The characteristics and uniqueness of banking services should inform the design and implementation of the methods of optimal solutions, in order to drive the efficient and effective functioning of banks and subsequently other organizations. The health of individual banks is essential to economic development, transformation and growth.

Bank failures are inevitable in an economy, and it would be unwise to aim for zero tolerance. The increased attention to corporate governance is aimed at minimizing corporate collapses, particularly bank failures as a result of controllable issues emanating mainly from the internal business environment. In view of banks being unique and complex adaptive systems, this section covers the methods of driving organizational effectiveness from a micro and macro perspective based on corporate governance deficiencies in the banking sector. The methods of optimal organizational effectiveness are also based on the stakeholder theory with special emphasis on the board, executive management, internal and external auditors, and regulatory authorities. These methods aim to address the corporate governance challenges in the preceding chapters. The methods of optimal solutions complement the rules-based approach to corporate governance by strengthening the internal structures, systems and process of the organization, and enhancing the feedback mechanisms from the internal and external environment; hence the necessity of organization development theory and practice as the prime solution to corporate challenges and change management. These methods support the evolution and disruption models in banking with a view to achieving organizational effectiveness as a result of effectively managing and controlling the technical and adaptive challenges prevalent in dynamic systems. These methods include risk governance, Decision Support Systems, HR Management Systems, Performance Measurement, Organization Learning, Management Innovation, and Corporate Meetings Alignment.

RISK GOVERNANCE

Risk management is an integral pillar to organizational effectiveness as it drives financial stability and solvency. Risk is inevitable in dynamic systems, as a result of the chaos characteristics of the modern organization. As elaborated in Chapter 9, most organizations and systems are high disorganized and unordered. Financial markets are characterized by volatile and ambiguous operating environment where the reactive actions taken by individuals alter and influence the outcome of certain events on both the manufacturing and distribution strategies. To ensure organizational effectiveness, the implementation of a risk management approach that identifies, assesses, analyzes, mitigates, monitors and report financial and non-financial risks is a necessity.

The risk governance framework should comprehensively define the responsibilities of board of directors, senior leaders and management. These responsibilities include: monitoring the control environment, reviewing and approving the management-developed strategy, and ensuring compliance of the institution with its legal and regulatory requirements. The risk governance methodologies should be premised on the four pillars of corporate governance, that is, accountability, fairness, transparency and responsibility. The Sarbanes Oxley Act of 2002 is an essential tool to enhancing the risk governance structure of an organization. Risk governance goes beyond mere critical study of complex, interacting networks in which choices and decisions are made. It encompasses a set of normative principles which inform all relevant actors of society on how to deal responsibly with risks.

In view of complexity science and Systems Thinking, the adoption of the Enterprise Risk Management framework is a necessity in enhancing sound corporate governance and subsequently organizational effectiveness in banks. Banks should focus their efforts on and beyond the four categories of business objectives: strategic, operations, reporting, and compliance. This requires the adoption of the connectivity matrix as a risk management tool in complex adaptive systems. A structured, holistic and integrative risk management approach based on systems thinking and Appreciative Inquiry should be adopted at all times in order to effectively identify and manage adaptations and interactions of risks. Risk convergence is essential in enhancing the risk management process and managing complexity risk in dynamic systems. This is a process of integrating different risk functions to streamline risk management. Converging risk management into an enterprise-wide framework will provide a platform to deliver the true picture of risk to the board and offers scope for significant cost saving. The 12 dimensions of the Burke-Litwin Model (*see Chapter 9*) can be used in enhancing the risk management of banks. The risk management methodologies of the bank should be strengthened by defining clearly the risk appetite and developing and updating the bank's risk profile. This should be supported by effective risk communication strategy. The risk governance methodologies should incorporate challenges that come with incorporating FinTech companies and incumbents because these high-tech companies are exacerbating complexity risk in the financial services sector. The challenges that emanate from the high-tech front runner companies include IT security and compatibility, regulatory uncertainty, required financial investment, contractual complexities, and differences in management and culture.

RegTech is essential in risk governance as it helps to characterize innovation and emerging technologies focused on solving complex regulatory challenges, enabling smarter regulation and reducing complexity in existing regulation and compliance. The board, C-suites and managers should be well-appraised of the risk governance methodologies in relation to the dynamic business environment.

DECISION SUPPORT SYSTEMS (DSS)

This is a collection of programs/software used for decision-making, particularly in complex adaptive systems. The adoption of Decision Support Systems and embracing the disruptive nature of FinTech as imperatives from growth and transformation signifies an appreciation by boards and senior executives of the role of Artificial Intelligence (AI) as a strategic corporate governance imperative. These programs help the board, executive leaders and management of organizations in planning, forecasting and managing all planned or emergent issues. Decision Support Systems usually include modeling capability that enables mathematical simulation of a situation in order to test various tactics, intelligence and strategies. The use of decision software helps to examine data and suggest an optimum decision or conclusion. Reliance on human decision making in dynamic systems creates the agency problem, hence the need to incorporate machine intelligence in corporate decisions. The implementation process of Decision

Support Systems can either be done by embedding Artificial Intelligence into systems with specific tasks (narrow AI), or building thinking machines with intelligence comparable to that of a human (Lauterbach and Bonime-Blanc, 2016).

Given the uniqueness and complexity of banking systems and operations, banks need to extensively invest in such business intelligence technologies as data analytics, mobile banking applications, Artificial Intelligence, cyber-security, robotics processes and automation, biometrics and identity management, distributed ledger technologies (such as blockchain), and public cloud infrastructure. Business Intelligence (BI) aims to support better business decision making in complex adaptive systems. This involves tools that are designed to retrieve, analyze, and report data. The Business Intelligence tools generally read data that has been previously stored, often in a data warehouse. This demands sound data management methodologies from collection, usage to data storage. The Business Intelligence concept helps to improve enterprise operation effectiveness and support management to achieve competitive advantages. Business Intelligence (BI) is "a set of concepts, methods, and technologies for turning separated yet related in-use-data in an organization into useful information in order to improve business performance." A Business Intelligence (BI) environment is characterized by Extracting, Transforming, and Loading (ETL) data into an Enterprise Data Warehouse (EDW). The data in the EDW is used for generating reports and queries across the organization. Business Intelligence technologies involve the following functions: reporting, online transaction processing (OLTP), online analytical processing (OLAP), analytics, data mining, process mining, complex event processing, business performance management, benchmarking, predictive analytics, and prescriptive analytics. These functions are pivotal to the effectiveness of dynamic organizations such as banking institutions. The integration of these various functions in the strategic and operational roadmaps of banks enables boards, C-suites and managers to gain a holistic view of an organization's problems, from which new insights can be derived and used to make predictions, monitor markets and manage risks. The key discovery and predictive categories of business intelligence tools that should be extensively used in complex adaptive systems such as banking are briefly explained below:

- *Spreadsheets* – mostly used in data presentation for sales, budgets and other numeric summaries. Spreadsheets are also useful in analyzing structured data. Organizations also use spreadsheets for data restructuring, aggregation, and general data analysis.
- *Reporting and Querying Software* – this involve tools that help to run regular reports, create organized listings, and perform cross-tabular reporting and querying.
- *Online Analytical Processing (OLAP)* - this Business Intelligence (BI) function involve technology used to perform complex analysis of data in a data warehouse. OLAP "enables analysts, managers and executives to gain insight into data through fast, consistent, interactive access to a wide variety of possible views of information that has been transformed from raw data to reflect the dimensionality of the enterprise." (OLAP Council). The three approaches for OLAP are Relational OLAP (ROLAP), Multi-dimensional OLAP (MOLAP), and Hybrid OLAP (ROLAP + MOLAP). ROLAP involve storing data in relational tables. MOLAP is used to store data in special structures called "Data cubes". The OLAP category provides the business with a good view of what is actually happening in the business at a specific time.
- *Dashboard* – this is an electronic interface that aggregates and visualizes data from multiple sources. The dashboard helps to monitor business performance and providing real-time information about the entire business or system performance. A dashboard provides in-depth business analysis, with a snapshot of each strategic business unit (SBU), trends and Key Performance Indicators (KPIs). The dashboard allows bank managers to monitor the contribution of various SBUs in their organization particularly in key functions such as IT,

152

Treasury, Lending, Risk, Retailing, and Compliance. A dashboard is classified as an Executive Information System (EIS) useful to garner business intelligence across all the business functions. It empowers users with the ability to see the significant evolutions, trends and relationships in business performance. Corporate governance should emphasize the cultivation of the requisite skills to interpret data on the data dashboard by all stakeholders.

- **Data Mining** – involves a combination of discovery and prediction techniques. Examples of data mining techniques that are relevant to banking are clustering, classification, association rules, frequent item-sets, and outlier detection. This category of Business Intelligence involves discovering patterns in large data sets involving methods at the intersection of machine learning, statistics, and database systems. It helps to find anomalies, hidden patterns and correlations within large data sets that characterize banking transactions. Data mining techniques also helps to improve fraud and risk detection accuracy and reduce the time spent on managing risk.

- **Data Warehousing** – this is the electronic storage of large amount of information by a business. This helps in the evaluation of the performance of the entire enterprise and that of individual Strategic Business Units (SBUs). The storage of data in a data warehouse is designed for query and analysis instead of mere transaction processing. The three main types of Data warehouse are Enterprise Data Warehouse (EDW), Operation Data Warehouse (ODW), and Data Mart.

- **Decision Engineering** – In view of the organization as complex adaptive system rather than a mechanistic, this framework is useful in unifying a number of alternatives for organizational decision making. Decision Engineering (DE) relies on a more structured and holistic approach to decision making. The framework is used to overcome decision making "complexity ceiling" which is characterized by a mismatch between the sophistication of organizational decision-making practices and the complexity of situations in which decisions must be made. The unified methodology of decision making adopts a systems thinking approach to deal with the complex internal and external business environment. Decision engineering practices involve requirements analysis, specification, scenario planning, quality assurance and security. Decision engineering approach is multi-disciplinary and makes use of findings on cognitive bias and decision making, situation awareness, critical and creative thinking, collaboration, and organization design. This is a solution to the increasingly dynamic business world in which the pace, scope and complexity of change are increasing.

- *Process Mining* – this is an important technique in process management and design thinking. This technique supports the analysis of business processes based on event logs. Process mining allows an organization to extract information from event logs and use the information in strategic decision making. The information from process mining is used to discover models; and describing processes, organizations and products that support the achievement of the organization's strategic intent. It is also useful in determining and monitoring any form of deviations in processes and products thereby ensuring strategic alignment. Other activities closely related to process mining include Business Activity Monitoring (BAM), Business Operations Management (BOM), and Business Process Improvement (BPI). In line with design thinking, process mining leads to a process model that represents current state operations based on hard evidence extracted from event logs. It is therefore useful in banking service design and the development of the banking service strategy and service portfolio.
- **Business Performance Management (BPM)** – This is a real-time system that alerts managers to potential opportunities, impending problems and threats, and then

empowers them to react through models and collaboration. BPM is also referred to as corporate performance management, enterprise performance management, or strategic enterprise management. BPM is an outgrowth of Business Intelligence and incorporates many of its technologies applications and techniques.

- *Local Information Systems* – this is a Business Intelligence (BI) tool designed to support geographic reporting and reporting at SBU level. In view of systems thinking the Local Information System of one unit should be integrated with all other units.

There are numerous Business Intelligence (BI) delivery mechanisms which should be used to enhance corporate governance and drive organizational effectiveness in banking. These Business Intelligence (BI) delivery mechanisms include:

- Scheduled reports
- Dashboards
- Trend Analysis Reports
- Forecasting
- Ad-Hoc/User Query Tools

HUMAN RESOURCE MANAGEMENT SUPPORT SYSTEMS

This represents a central repository of employee data useful in organizational development. Human Resource Management System is an integrated system used to gather, store and analyze information regarding an organization's human resources (Hedrickson, 2003). This includes systems, people, policies and procedures used to manage the HR function in an organization. This is made possible through Enterprise Resource Planning (ERP). Enterprise Resource Planning (ERP) is essential in integrating several data sources into a unified system. Effective performance management solutions can improve the following areas in an organization:

- Employee goal planning
- Career development

- Competency assessment
- Performance appraisal
- Payroll and Compensation management
- Organization strategic alignment

These human resource management areas help to ensure employee engagement, commitment and innovativeness; thereby enhancing the organization's self-organizing capacity. "No company, small or large, can win over the long run without energized employees who believe in the firm's mission and understand how to achieve it. That's why you need to take the measure of employee engagement at least once a year through anonymous surveys in which people feel completely safe to speak their minds" (Jack and Suzy Welch, n.d). Engaged and committed employees, through their discretionary efforts gives their firms crucial competitive advantage, plus increased productivity and lower staff turnover. Employee engagement entails the extent to which employees fully occupy themselves in their daily tasks and the strength of their commitment to the company and their roles (Vance, 2006).

Commitment is generally defined as "a willingness to persist in a course of action and reluctance to change plans, owing to a sense of obligation to stay the course" (Vance, 2006). It manifests itself through intentionally devoting extra time and energy to fulfill job responsibilities. The emotional component of commitment ensures people experience and express positive feelings toward an entity they work for. Commitment is also based on reason as employees consciously choose to make commitments, then they thoughtfully plan and carry out the actions that yield positive results.

To ensure employees get engaged and generate valuable business results, organizations should adopt such practices as job design, recruitment & selection, employee training & development, compensation, performance management and career development.

Various researchers have identified commitment as an important factor to increase innovative behavior in organization (Agarwal, 2014; Kehoe and Wright, 2013). Employees' commitment towards an organization includes their desire to see the company succeed. Employee commitment acts as intrinsic motivation that trigger innovative behavior as commitment provokes the willingness of employees to dedicate discretionary behaviors and efforts beyond contractual terms towards outcomes desired by the organization. In order to stay competitive, workforce innovative behavior is of paramount importance. "Creativity is vital to the health of firms in today's knowledge economy, as only by fostering the innovative behavior of their employees can firms obtain and maintain competitive advantages" (Niu, 2014). Organizations today operate in a highly dynamic and flexible environment where generating a competitive advantage is vital for survival (Prieto and Perez-Santana, 2014). Competitive advantage can be achieved through differentiation or lower costs. Employees' innovative behavior results in lower costs due to process improvements or differentiation from competitors due to innovative products. This makes innovative employees an imperative for organizations. Employees' knowledge and attitudes towards the business and the organizational goals can be critical for a successful innovation and a resulting competitive advantage (Kehoe and Wright, 2003).

Innovative behavior can be defined as the new, intentional and beneficial ideas created, introduced and applied to everyday actions within a group or organization (Niu, 2014; Prieto and Perez-Santana, 2014). Employees can use their innovative behavior to improve job processes, procedures, methods and operations (Prieto and Perez-Santana, 2014). "An engaged workforce is considered to be a cornerstone of sustaining a competitive advantage" (Agarwal, 2014). Companies that intend to improve their competitive position through innovations need to focus on the ideas of employees to identify areas of improvement (Scott and Bruce, 1994) based on employees' knowledge, creativity and attitude towards the organization with a special focus on everyday turbulences and opportunities faced. Innovative behavior is also defined as the result of intrinsic and extrinsic motivation of employees (Hammond, Neff, Farr, Schwall and Zhao, 2011; Prieto and Perez-Santana, 2014). Intrinsic motivation refers to an individual's inner engagement and commitment to the task and extrinsic to factors outside of the task (Hammond *et al.,* 2011), such as financial rewards.

PERFORMANCE MEASUREMENT

This is a system that assists managers in tracking the implementation of business strategy by comparing actual results against strategic goals and objectives. It involves clear definition of outcomes and driver Key Performance Indicators (KPIs). A KPI represents a strategic objective and metrics that measures performance against a goal. KPIs cover operational areas such as customer performance, service performance, sales operations, and sales forecasts. The use of Business Intelligence mechanisms is a necessity in overall business performance measurement. Performance measurement helps to focus the attention of organizational members on a common objective and galvanize them towards the attainment of the objectives.

Contemporary businesses are expected to focus on not only the economic measures or responsibilities but to incorporate legal, ethical and philanthropic responsibilities that cover societal norms, or standards. Banks must recognize and respond to environmental changes as determined by industry trends, market structure, competition, and public expectations in terms of terms of the societal and ethical performance. Carroll (1970) emphasized the increasing importance of examining corporations not just on their accounting or market-based success, but also on non-economic criteria. This is in line with the Triple Bottom Line reporting requirement in which firms should report on people, planet and profit. The performance management system should therefore be integrative and structured to incorporate all these elements.

ORGANIZATIONAL LEARNING

Organizational learning is a practice that all organizations need to adopt in order to ensure organizational effectiveness. The banking sector is characterized by enormous disruptive changes which demands unmatched combinations of quality, innovation, efficiency, and customization in order to deliver value. These new sources of value in the banking space require individual banks to avoid the familiar and enhance the capacity to self-renew through adaptation. Banking customers have become knowledgeable and expect nothing short of high quality, customization, convenience, and timeliness. The most fundamental strategic capability to deal with the disruptive and wrenching changes in the business environment is "an organization's propensity to learn, that is, to acquire, apply, and spread new insights." (Fiol and Lyles, 1985). The prioritization of organizational learning will enable banking institutions to generate innovations, adapt to changing environments, take advantage of emergent market opportunities and create competitive advantage. Banks should increase the focus on competition, markets, customers, and commitment to employees. These should be the strategic areas for internal corporate governance because organizational learning enhances the ability to explore, interpret, revise old approaches, develop new knowledge, and allowing systems to self-organize.

Organizational learning is the process through which an organization gains insight and understanding about the interdependence and interaction of its internal and external environment. Organizations as complex adaptive systems should mimic complexity principles in their structure and operations. This should be supported by the Business Intelligence (BI) tools such as data mining, decision engineering, and process mining. Organizations learn through experience, experimentation, observation, analysis and through critically examining successes and failures. The process of organizational learning emphasizes making and updating routines (recurrent sequences of action) in response to experiences and empowering bottom-up and emergent processes. These routines include "organizational roles, rules, conventions, strategies, structures, technologies, cultural practices, and capabilities" (Levitt and March, 1988). The process mining and data mining methodologies support this process of updating routines. Organizational learning is an essential method of optimal corporate governance because the strategic capability of an organization is reflected in the competencies and dynamic capabilities, organizational knowledge and strategic skills, continuous improvement, diagnosis of strategic capability and development of strategic capabilities (Ljubojevic *et al.,* 2013). Through organizational learning, corporate governance should ensure the following organizational learning vowels of organizational effectiveness:

	Action	Explanations
A	**Analyze**	The organization should make decisions based on detailed analysis and consensus from all stakeholders. This should be based on Online Analytical Process (OLAP), digital dashboard, reporting and querying methodologies.
E	**Evaluate**	The changing business environment requires an evaluation of alternatives in decision making. Decision engineering is useful in the evaluation of alternatives.
I	**Improve**	The organization should constantly improve its products and services. This should be based on dashboard data, spreadsheets, and other Business Intelligence delivery mechanisms.

O	Offer	The organization should offer its stakeholders opportunities to grow with it. The OD principles are essential in this respect.
U	Update	The organization should constantly revise and modernize its methods of doing business – procedures, processes, and systems. This can be operationalized through organizational reengineering and OD principles and practices.

Adapted from Justine Chinoperekweyi, Unpublished Ph.D Thesis

The above vowels help in the process of co-evolution of internal edges of chaos and the pervasive external sustainability dilemmas in organizations. The ability to learn and change fast is a source of competitive advantage. Organizations should therefore adopt complexity principles such as self-organization, non-linear feedback, edge of chaos, co-evolution, emergence, and path dependence. According to complexity researchers, these interventions support unhindered cross-channel communication, sanction conversations across boundaries, enables productive energy to be directed to key issues, support the formation of collaborative networks, facilitate bottom-up processes, and assist in the translation of new innovations from one context into others.

ORGANIZATIONAL REENGINEERING

The continuous adaptation and co-evolution that takes place between organizations and the environment results in the emergence of conflicts between processes in complex adaptive systems. The resultant conflict between activities require that organizations adopt external controls to effectively expedite the formation of new schema. This can be done through reengineering thereby rectifying emergent schemas in organizations. Schema refers to norms, values, beliefs, and assumptions that are shared among the collective. Reengineering is critical to strategic alignment and to the attainment of business results due to organization dynamism and the networked relationships of the organization. Reengineering should be a part of every modern-day banking institution in order to ensure strategic flexibility through consistency and reliability. Reengineering is the fundamental rethinking and radical redesign of business processes to achieve dramatic improvements in a critical quantum leap of contemporary measure of performance (Hammer and Champy, 1993). This requires a great deal of process-oriented managers, rather than relying on managers who focus mainly on tasks, on jobs, on people, on structures, and on themselves. A business process is a collection of activities that takes inputs and creates an output. Reengineering drives strategic flexibility, transforms the business and minimizes the agency problem as managers stop acting like the 1924 Hawthorne supervisors and start behaving like coaches. Workers shift focus from their bosses to customers.

The increasing banking disruptive evolutions and revolutions require process orientation and creative optimal use of information technology in order to cope with ambiguity and realize valuable opportunities. The business environment has become fast paced and highly unpredictable to box people in some standard procedures without driving engagement, learning, collaboration, change, and ensuring the workforce sees the future. The reengineering process requires that banks engage Education Specialists rather than Trainers, to oversee talent, culture, performance, and change issues towards the attainment of strategic goals and objectives.

There are different names given to reengineering, such as redesign of core processes, process innovation, redesigning business processes, organization reengineering. It involves starting everything from the beginning rather than perpetuating the old methods of doing business. Reengineering therefore leads to the development of new business models. It involves changing the organization's strategies, change in organizational structure, simplification, and change in process, skills, and behaviors.

In view of increased competition and globalization, Business Process Reengineering (BPR) can bring incredible solutions to businesses or complex adaptive systems. BPR produces positive results for firms in critical contemporary measures of performance such as cost, productivity, service, customer satisfaction, and speed. BPR has a strategic value in managing organizational change as it includes new vision or strategy: a need to build operational capabilities, need to reevaluate strategic options, enter new markets or redefine products/services (Thyagarajan and Khatibi, 2004). This process is driven from the top and requires conceptual skills, strategic thinking and constant commitment. BPR is "the ability to rethink, restructure and streamline the business structures, process, methods of working management systems and external relationships through which we create and deliver value" (Talwar, 1993). The fundamental elements of BPR are process redesign, value addition, integration of cross-functional specialization, and exploitation of IT. These elements are premised on design thinking hence the necessity of management innovation.

Business Process Reengineering (BPR) Essential Tools and Techniques

- *Process visualization* – this involve creating a clear vision of the process o be engineered. This is important in smoothening the banking service strategy given the fragmented elements of the banking service delivery system. This demands process knowledge at different levels of the system.
- *Process mapping and modelling* – encompasses process flowcharting, and role activity diagramming. These provide a graphical representation of the business process in view of the roles, responsibilities and standards. The modelling process helps to provide a visual way to understand, analyze and improve upon methods of working. Process mapping helps in

identifying relationships between processes and elements such as strategies, business capabilities and roles.

- *Change management* – the success of BPR lies on effective change management, especially the human element of reengineering. This is in view of the volatility of the business operating environment. Change management is at the center of the business process reengineering.

- *Benchmarking* – benchmarking helps in visualization and development of the processes. This helps in determining requirements and setting goals. It involves searching for the "best practice" to drive superior performance. Examples include performance benchmarking, process benchmarking, internal and competitive benchmarking.

- *Problem-solving and Diagnosis* – Pareto diagramming, and cognitive mapping

- *Process measurement* – involves Activity-based costing and statistical process control. It involves process monitoring, control and operational analysis.

- *Process and customer focus* – BPR involve redesigning the process in order to enhance customer satisfaction

- *Project management* – involve budgeting and project scheduling. The main functions of project management are leading, planning, organizaing and controlling.

The successful implementation of BPR requires: "(1) consistency between the company's business strategy and vision, and a clear understanding of customer, market, industry, and competitive directions, (2) a management commitment to implement fundamentally different ways of conducting business, (3) a business case that is founded on proven analytical approaches, (4) a project team with the capacity to evolve from simply conceptualizing change to actually developing and implementing it" (Farell, 1994).

MANAGEMENT INNOVATION

The bank failures explained in the introduction chapter resulted partly from the focus on management qualities that do not build resilient and inventive organizations. These qualities that do not create value, yet are highly rewarded in organizations include: self-discipline, economy, orderliness, rationality, prudence, reliability, moderation, fastidiousness. In a world of wrenching change, the most valuable human capabilities are precisely those that are least manageable: nerve, artistry, elan, originality, grit, non-conformity, valor, and derring-do.

Corporate governance should ensure the existence of organizations capable of spontaneous renewal. Management innovation ensures that the electric current of innovation pulses through every activity of the organization and the renegades trump the reactionaries. Management innovation is the invention and implementation of a management practice, process, structure, or technique that is new to the state of the art and is intended to further organizational goals (Birkinshaw *et al.,* 2008). Organizations need to develop well-honed methodologies for product innovation through the formation of R&D groups that explore the frontiers of science and leveraging on digital providers/FinTech. Management innovation requires the prioritization of the positive and negative influences of Artificial Intelligence in the organization's strategic and operational road maps. The governance mechanism of modern banks should be guided by an understanding of the challenges and opportunities that are attached to the incorporation Artificial Intelligence (AI) into the organization's systems.

There are four main perspectives in management innovation: an institutional perspective, fashion perspective, cultural perspective and a rational perspective. The institutional perspective focuses on the socio-economic conditions that shape management ideas and practices (Guillen, 1994). A fashion perspective deals with the dynamic interplay between users and providers of management ideas

(Abrahamson, 1996). The cultural perspective deals with how the organization reacts to new ideas and management practices (Zbaracki, 1998). A rational perspective focuses on how management innovations and their implementation are undertaken (Chandler, 1962).

MEETINGS ALIGNMENT

The modern corporation has assumed a dominant position in today's highly globalized society. As a social construction the corporation is made up of different components and functional areas which should be coordinated in order to ensure synergy and achievement of the overall strategic intent. Organizational effectiveness is a product of effective synergy, adaptation, goal-orientation and coordinated balance between the different functions and levels of an organization. Effective meetings and meetings alignment are instruments for organizational effectiveness. Organizations with coordinated meetings across the organization's hierarchy exhibit strength in leadership, decision-making, people, work processes, systems, and culture. An understanding of the ingredients, incentives, and integration mechanism of the different categories of corporate meetings is essential in collaborative working, competency building, collaborative leadership, community building, creative leadership, change leadership, and capacity building at each level of the organization.

Meetings are an essential tool for strategic alignment and as such the integration of meetings is fundamental to the sustainability of banking institutions. Integrated and effective organizations posses significant financial and social benefits to economies. Meetings and meetings alignment plays an important role in driving organizational effectiveness.

The emergence of conglomerate structures, effects of globalization, and the intensity of competition in all markets call for a study in corporate meetings alignment in relation to organizational effectiveness. There has been an increase in corporate failures, corporate governance deficiencies, project failures, and corporate conflicts in most countries during the past two decades, yet effective meetings can produce lasting solutions. Most organizations exhibit the characteristics of the bureaucratic organization as developed by Max Weber (1864-1920). These characteristics include degree of division of labor, well-defined chain of command, formal relationships between organizational members, well-defined rules and regulations, and recruitment based on qualifications. To counter the bureaucratic organization's criticism on hampered coordination and communication, meetings alignment is essential.

To ensure organizational effectiveness corporate meetings should be conducted in terms of a strategic process where certain responsibilities and specific behaviors determine the achievement of corporate goals. In line with the organization's hierarchy, the three major strategic processes responsibilities are creation, translation, and execution (Phillips, 2011). Corporate executives are primarily responsible to create the plan, managers are responsible to translate the plan and make it meaningful and comprehensible to all employees, and front-line employees are responsible to execute the plan (Phillips, 2011).

The organization is a collective unit comprising internal and external stakeholders. There is collaboration and harmonious working relationship between all constituencies of the social structure. Though the exercise of power and authority exists in line with the hierarchical structure, the collaborative structure proposed in this model is essential for organizational effectiveness. The interaction of the different constituencies of the organization can either be formal or informal. The alignment of all the six constituencies is fundamental to this model. The GSM is primarily concerned with the vision of the organization whilst the board of directors is responsible for developing the strategy, strategic thinking, and strategic leadership. In line with the leader centrality construct, the GSM is considered the core of the interaction. The executive committee is responsible for policy, process, and resource recommendations whilst the management meeting focuses on planning, organizing, reporting, and execution of strategic plans. The Board meetings play a bridging role between the leader and everyone else in the organization. Staff meetings focus on the operational issues of the organization and acts as the contact point for stakeholder engagement. Stakeholder engagement meetings focus on collaboration and shared decision making with all the people or firms who have an interest in the organization. This is in line with the corporate community model and the objective of creating shared value (Porter, 2013).

BIBLIOGRAPHY

Abdallah, H. and Valentine, B. (2009) Fundamentals and Ethics Theories of Corporate Governance. *Middle Eastern Finance and Economics.* **4**, pp. 88-96.

Acharya, V. V. and Schnabl, P. (2009) *Do global banks spread global imbalances? The case of asset-backed commercial paper during the financial crisis of 2007–2009.* Working Paper, New York University: Stern School of Business.

Akkermans, H. A. and Oorschot, K. E. (2004) Relevance Assumed: A Case Study of Balanced Scorecard Development Using System Dynamics. *Journal of the Operational Research Society*, July, pp. 23-31.

Alchian, A. and Demsatz, H. (1972) Production, information costs, and economic organization. *American Economic Review.* **62**(5), pp. 777-795.

Ashmos, D. P. and Duchon, D. (2000) Spirituality at work: A conceptualization and measure. *Journal of Management Inquiry.* **9**(2), pp. 134-44

Athanasoglou, P., Delis, M. and Staikouras, C. (2006) Determinants in the bank profitability in the South Eastern European Region. *Journal of Financial Decision Making.* **2**(1), pp. 1-17.

Bain, J. (1968) *Industrial Organization.* John Wiley and Sons, New York.

Boyd, B. (1991) Strategic Planning and Financial Performance: A Meta-Analytic Review. *Journal of Management Studies.* **28**(4), pp. 353-374.

Cadbury, A. (1992) *Report on the Committee on the Financial Aspects of Corporate Governance*. Gee: London.

Cadbury, A. (2000) *Global Corporate Governance Forum*. UK: World Bank

Cadbury, A. (2002) *Corporate Governance and Chairmanship: A Personal View*. Oxford: Oxford Press.

Cadbury, A. (2002) The Corporate Governance Agenda. *Corporate Governance*. **8**(1), pp. 7-15.

Calomiris, C. W. (2007) *Bank Failures in Theory and History: The Great Depression and Other Contagious Events*. NBER Working Paper No. 13597.

Calomiris, C. W. and Khan, C. M. (1991) The role of demandable debt in structuring optimal banking arrangements. *American Economic Review*. **81**(3), pp. 497–513.

Carroll, A. B. (1979) A three-dimensional model of corporate performance. *Academy of Management Review*. 4(4), pp. 497-505.

Carroll, A. B. (2000). The four faces of corporate citizenship. *Business Ethics*, McGraw-Hill: Guilford, pp. 187-91.

Chinoperekweyi, J. (2018) *Decision Making for Transformational Presence: Guide to making decisions that work*. India: Notion Press Publishing

Chinoperekweyi, J. (2018) Harnessing OD theory, practice and interventions as a strategic imperative for organizational effectiveness. IOD. Florida-USA

Denis, D. K. and McConnell, J. J. (2003) International Corporate Governance. *Journal of Financial and Quantitative Analysis*. **38**(1), pp. 1-36.

Denzin, N. K. and Lincoln, Y. S. (2003) *The landscape of qualitative research*. Thousand Oaks, CA: Sage.

Freeman R. E. (1984) *Strategic Management: A Stakeholder approach.* US, Boston: Pitman.

Galbraith, J. R. (2002) Designing Organizations: An Executive Guide to Strategy, Structure, and Processes. San Francisco: Jossey-Bass Publishers.

Knell, A. (2006) *Corporate governance, how to add value to your company: A practical implementation guide.* Oxford: Elsevier.

McConvill, J. (2005) Positive Corporate Governance and its Implications for Executive Compensation. *German Law Journal.* **12**(6), pp. 1777-1804.

Mehran, H. and Mollineaux, L. (2012) *Corporate Governance of Financial Institutions.* Federal Reserve Bank of New York Staff Reports. Staff Report no. 539

Mehran, H., Morrison, A. and Shapiro, J. (2011) *Corporate Governance and Banks: What Have We Learned from the Financial Crisis?* Federal Reserve Bank of New York Staff Reports. Staff Report no. 502

Mintzberg H. (1983) *Power In and Around Organizations.* Englewood Cliffs, New Jersey: Prentice Hall.

Mintzberg, H. (1979) Structure in 5's: A synthesis of the research on organization design. *Management Science.* **26**(3), pp. 322-341.

Monks, R. A. G. and Minow, N. (1995) *Corporate governance.* Cambridge, MA: Blackwell.

Morck, R, Shleifer, A. and Vishney, R. W. (1989) Alternative Mechanisms for Corporate Control, *American Economic Review.* **79**(4), pp. 842-52.

Porter, M. E. and Kramer, M. R. (2011) Creating Shared Value: How to reinvent capitalism- and unleash a wave of innovation and growth. *Harvard Business Review.* **January/February 2011**(3), pp. 63-70

Shah, S. N. (2014) *The principal-agent problem in finance(a summary).* CFA Institute Research Foundation

Shahin, A. and Zairi, M. (2007) Corporate governance as a critical element for driving excellence in corporate social responsibility. *International Journal of Quality and Reliability Management.* **24**(7), pp. 753-770.

Shiller, R. J. (2008) *The Subprime Solution: How Today's Global Financial Crisis Happened and What to Do about It.* Princeton, New Jersey: Princeton University Press.

Solomon, J. and Solomon, A. (2004) *Corporate governance and accountability.* Chichester: Wiley.

Spanos, L. J. (2005) Corporate Governance in Greece: Developments and Policy Implications. *Corporate Governance.* **5**(1), pp. 15-30.

Walker, L. W. (1999) Governing Board: Know Thyself: Self Assessment is the Basis for High Performance. *Trustee.* **52**(8), pp. 14-19.

Watkins, K. E. and Marsick, V. J. (1997) *Dimensions of the learning organization.* Warwick, RI: Partners for the Learning Organization.

INDEX

www.ingramcontent.com/pod-product-compliance
Lightning Source LLC
Chambersburg PA
CBHW020902180526
45163CB00007B/2600